REST AND RISE

Be Refreshed In Your Work

4-Week Bible Study

KASEY SHULER

Three Verses to Pray Each Day

You can find rest in Jesus without doing hours of study or skipping sleep. For the days when the 5 am quiet time club is not in the cards, download a printable template with three Scriptures to pray before your day!

You can access this resource at kaseybshuler.com/3verses.

www.kaseybshuler.com

To my mom, who inspires me to
live life to the full.

Table of
CONTENTS

INTRODUCTION

God invited us to be fruitful and multiply goodness. I believe we have a desire to fulfill this great calling in our lives, but a focus on work isn't working.

We all need rest, but we we aren't taking it. Americans lose $223 billion in unused vacation days.[1] Hustling through our breaks not only costs dollars, but leaves us feeling overworked or unworthy. Even if we use every spare moment to be productive, go to bed late, get up early, and put in our best effort day after day, it's not enough. By the time the weekend rushes in, we still feel behind and our efforts are unacknowledged. The weight of work can feel unbearable.

Here's the good news:
Once we learn how to rest in Jesus, He will multiply our work.

Instead of leaning on our own strength, God invites us to do work His way. Over the next four weeks, we will dig deep into Matthew 11:28-30. Jesus will teach us how to rest so we can rise with a renewed perspective, be refreshed with His presence, and accomplish greater things than we ever could on our own.

---

[1] Andrew Soergel, "By Skipping Your Vacation You're Hurting America," U.S. *News and World Report.* June 17, 2016. https://www.usnews.com/news/articles/2016-06-17/study-unused-vacation-days-drag-on-economy.

If you live with aching ambitions, deferred dreams, and stress headaches, this study is for you. If you long for both satisfaction in your work and a day at the spa, you're in the right place!

As a personal trainer, I used to measure progress by the amount of squats, sweat, and weight lost. My clients enjoyed the results for a time, but there was still something missing. One day, a friend pointed out a picture of an athlete's face as he crossed the finish line in record time: it was a look of pure serenity. This athlete had learned to rest *in* his work. He trained to adapt his body to any level of stress and quickly return his heart rate to homeostasis. My own clients suffered from the stress of jobs, kids, family, and responsibilities. What they yearned for was not just a thinner frame or faster mile but stability, balance, and resilience in their daily lives.

We do not need more burpees; we need to learn how to breathe.

Once I recognized the power of the ability to rest in any situation, I changed my training methods. I started and ended each session with this prayer over my clients: "Lord, as we rest in You, may You move in us." My clients worked harder and took more risks because they began their workout from a place of soul rest. Their perspective shifted from working to get it right to moving because they are already loved. And bonus: the exercise equipped them to adapt better to daily stress.

This rest and rise cycle makes us not just physically fit but spiritually ready in every moment of impending anxiety, pounding pressure, or weighty decision-making. Ashley, a client and CEO of a photography business based in Georgia, says,

"I have found that the rest and rise method helps me be more attuned to the true goodness that God has in store for my life. Instead of feeling the pressure to create my own way, I experience freedom through following His path. Resting my plans in God first has proved to be richer than anything I could have created for myself."

As you go to Jesus in this study of His Word, He will restore you. He is faithful, and His Word never returns empty. This study will train you to acknowledge your needs so He can fill you with peace for every circumstance and strengthen you to do the Father's will.

I don't want you to spend any more time in a depleting cycle of working for rest when you can experience rest right in the middle of your work. As you walk through this study, you will sow seeds of eternal significance in your life and those around you. As the saying goes: when is the best time to plant a tree? Twenty-five years ago. The second best time is today.

I wish I would have started twenty-five years ago. I want you to find rest today.

The Source of My Dysfunction and Jesus' Answer

A few years ago, a physical therapist delivered a diagnosis. It changed my life, or rather, defined my past.

I was incapable of physical relaxation from years of chronic striving.

I made an appointment to fix something called diastasis recti, which is a separation of the abdominal walls. It occurred during pregnancy, but unfortunately it did not resolve after birth or by any Google diagnostic.

Instead of teaching me some new kind of plank, my physical therapist told me to relax. I did. She told me to try again, but I couldn't do it, and I couldn't believe it! Even though I felt relaxed, the muscles were still tense. Like so many other parts of my life, I was relying on my own strength to hold it all together.

I remember a high school friend teaching me a six-pack abs trick: if you tighten your abs at all times, you work them all day and will therefore get a six-pack. She failed to inform me they would stay that way. She didn't know that a chronically tight abdominal wall doesn't allow for diaphragmatic breathing, proper oxygen flow, and relaxation to the body and brain.

If the muscles can't relax, my therapist explained, they can't pull back to generate as much force for a muscle contraction, hindering my full range of movement and weakening the muscle infrastructure.

They key to great movement starts with the ability to rest.

I was operating under this assumption: you work, then are rewarded with rest. You get the paycheck so you can pay for

Netflix. You workout so you can eat, right?

I discovered a few holes in this plot. Just like my abs, I couldn't let things go. I felt like I was constantly working to hold everything together. But instead of keeping me whole, this pride and fear-filled belief pulled me apart...literally.

This began changing for me when I published a project I had been working hard on and didn't receive the response I was looking for. When I heard crickets from others, another voice filled the silence. It was an echo of my go-getter mom's mantra from my childhood: *You can rest when you're dead.* This was something she would say casually, but my sixteen-year-old self took it seriously. I didn't know it until then, but I had been living by this phrase most of my life. That's why I could never relax—I didn't give myself permission to rest until the work was complete. But the work is never done!

However, this time the voice was different. It was the voice of a Father putting his kid to sleep at night—like God saying to me, "You can rest now. Jesus died, and when you put your faith in His life, you died to your old ways of striving. You can rest in Me now. Rest in my strength. Receive my love. I hold you together. You don't have to do anything to prove yourself. The work of salvation is finished."

When I heard those words it was like my shoulders melted. I didn't realize how tightly I held them. For once, I felt free to just sit still and receive, to be okay not doing anything, to feel what it was like to be held together by what Jesus has done instead of what I do.

I'm telling you this because I don't want you, or anyone else, to find themselves at a doctor's office because you burned out your adrenals, or can't sleep at night. I don't want you to sink into discouragement because you built something grand and people did not come. You may feel overworked and unworthy by the measure of this world, but Jesus says otherwise.

Background on the Text

"Come to me, all who labor and are heavy laden, and I will give you rest. Take my yoke upon you, and learn from me, for I am gentle and lowly in heart, and you will find rest for your souls. For my yoke is easy, and my burden is light."
Matthew 11:28-30 ESV

In Matthew 11:28-30, Jesus invites us to come to Him, find rest by working with Him, and to reap a harvest of righteousness—a prize that cannot be lost in a financial recession, stolen from underneath you, forgotten, or moth-eaten. What we build in Christ will stand forever. He will accomplish His will, and we get to be a part of that. No more gray hair over dusty plaques, no more broken relationships over failed businesses, no more blood money for empires of sand.

When we rest in the love of God, we will rise in steadfast purpose.

This explicit invitation to rest is only recorded in the book of Matthew, a book intended to prove to the Jews that Jesus Christ was the promised Messiah. Matthew was a tax collector, a profession that was generally disdained by the public. He felt the burden of societal norms. He wanted the Jewish people to accept Jesus as He was instead of the political king they wanted Him to be. Matthew wanted to spread the news: the gospel revolution turns the status quo upside down.

In Matthew 11:28-30, Jesus addresses the legalism of the

Pharisees, who sit in the judgement seat of Moses[2]. These religious leaders broke down the Ten Commandments into hundreds of "more practical" rules and degraded anyone who could not follow them.

Then God shows up.

And instead of Jesus saying, "Well done, my good and faithful Pharisees. You have policed this nation to my liking, so the people do exactly as I say," He says, "Woe to you lawyers as well! For you weigh men down with burdens hard to bear, while you yourselves will not even touch the burdens with one of your fingers'" (Luke 11:46). Then Jesus turns to the people, the ones who keep breaking His commandments, and says, "Come to me."

Come to me, student who is tired of playing by the rules.

Come to me, weary mom who serves everyone else before herself.

Come to me, employee who feels like their work never pays off.

"Are you tired? Worn out? Burned out on religion? Come to me. Get away with me and you'll recover your life. I'll show you how to take a real rest. Walk with me and work with me—watch how I do it. Learn the unforced rhythms of grace. I won't lay anything heavy or ill-fitting on you. Keep company with me and you'll learn to live freely and lightly." Matthew 11, The Message

---

[2] Matthew 23:2

HOW TO GET THE MOST OUT OF THIS STUDY

What do you hope to learn or take away from this study?

Will you go through this study on your own or with someone else? Be sure to tag #restandrisestudy with your journey so we can learn from one another and support each other.

I pre-program my coffee so it's waiting for me next to my Bible study at the kitchen table. I like to imagine that Jesus is waiting there for me too. When and where do you plan to do this study?

For those who are in a group study, let's lay out the purpose and expectations for your your *Rally* time. The *Rally* is communal time to reflect, grow, and hold each other accountable to resting and rising.

- *Rally* is a place to feel safe and loved.
- We don't need to fix each other. We get to listen, use words for building up others, and let the Lord do His work.
- Everything shared stays within the group.
- God is after our hearts. He waits on us. We get to reciprocate by showing up, doing the work, and being honest.

Go team!

OVERVIEW

N ow that our mind is thoroughly warmed-up and intentions are clear, let's get down to how we will walk through this study with the Lord. Our method for beginning each day is based on one simple but profound rhythm: resting and rising.

REST

In this section, we will surrender our own ways of striving and give them to the Lord, taking His yoke upon us.

While our typical day starts with the sun, the Jewish calendar begins with the nightfall. When God created each day, He declared, "and there was evening and there was morning, the first day" (Genesis 1:5b). Adam came to life because of God's exhale. Similarly, we receive the Spirit through faith upon Christ's exhale, His final breath, on the cross: "When Jesus had received the sour wine, he said, 'It is finished,' and he bowed his head and gave up his spirit" (John 19:30).

We will begin each day of study with rest, with a posture of humility before the Lord, in acknowledgement that our day, our work—our very life—begins with Him. We will spend time in prayer, thanking the Lord for what He has done and who He is in our life. After giving thanks, we lay down our cares before

Him in pen and prayer. Finally, we will give an offering of silence to declare that we are listening. This silence serves to create space between the anxieties that press in on us so we can press into the Lord.

Practicing silence will be hard at first. We will start small with a minute of silence, and by the end of the study we will not only endure, but enjoy, twelve full minutes of being still in the Lord's presence. Practicing this spiritual discipline is not only beneficial for our relationship with God, but for our bodies and relationships with others. In the book "What Your Body Knows About God,"[3] Rob Moll shares this research on prayer and its effects on our physiological system and relationships:

"Twelve minutes of attentive and focused prayer every day for eight weeks changes the brain significantly enough to be measured in a brain scan. Not only that, but it strengthens areas of the brain involved in social interaction, increasing our sense of compassion and making us more sensitive to other people. It also reduces stress, bringing another measurable physical effect— lower blood pressure. Prayer in this deeper, more attentive way also strengthens the part of the brain that helps us override our emotional and irrational urges."

Practicing silence is like learning how to do a squat; the first time it may seem awkward, but over time, will feel more natural and help support your daily movements. Once we can learn how to be silent for a length of time, we will find ourselves retreating into this space of inner peace in our most desperate moments of unrest.

---

[3] Rob Moll, *What Your Body Knows About God: How We are Designed to Connect, Serve And Thrive* (Illinois, IVP Books, 2014), 15.

Upon entering this space of silence, be prepared for your mind to continue running. Listen for the gentle voice of the Father whispering, "Hush," like a dad to his daughter. Allow the Spirit to rest upon you and settle you with peace. We have the permission and ability to cease from our striving because the work of salvation is finished. As we exhale deeply, let us surrender our lives to our Savior, let go of what we think we know, and be open to receive from the Lord.

Go to kaseybshuler.com/shop/restandrisestudy for a video of the Rest meditation.

REFLECT

As a worker surveys a field, *Reflect* will help you survey your life as it relates to rest and fruitfulness. Consider your current circumstances as the weather, where there could be clear skies today and a storm tomorrow. Test your thoughts as the soil, whose quality makes the difference between a scarce and abundant harvest. Humble your heart with Scripture as a plow to break up the hard ground to make room for seed. And as a team of oxen share the burden of the plow, surrender to the Lord and move in His perfect purpose for the field.

Don't worry about getting the "right" answer. When studying Scripture, pray first. Surrender your thoughts for the mind of Christ. Then ask these questions:

- What does it say?
- What does it mean?
- How can I respond?

Ask the Lord for wisdom[4], be attentive to any answer He might give you through Scripture or the Spirit, and discuss your question in community as you rally at the end of the week.

We will take time to walk slowly through the text, asking new questions and finding answers we didn't know were there. Don't get discouraged if you fall behind. This study does not exist for you to fill in all the blank spaces but to create space for you and the Lord. If that means you spend all our time with Him on two questions, wrestling with tangled roots of the past, you're doing it right.

We will discover more about who God is, and thus who we are: beloved by the maker of the sun and seasons, image-bearers and children made to enjoy His gifts by stewarding them. In doing so, we will prepare for a great harvest!

RISE

After starting each day with rest, we reflect on Scripture and then rise with purpose. We have joined with the Lord under his yoke, assessed the work, and now it's time to move! *Rise* is an opportunity for you to work out what you have gained from Scripture and prayer.

The sun rises everyday without ceasing. It does not rise for the applause of man; neither does it cease to rise amidst a gray sky threatening to cloud its presence. The sun rises because the Lord set it in motion at the beginning of time, and its endless rhythm gives glory to God and the certainty of a schedule for us.

---

[4] James 1:5

The rest and rise cycle mimics this wheel in the sky. The circular image we will refer to for our cycle is the two-wheeled plow.

As the oxen move, the top of the wheel rolls forward into a resting position on the ground, then rises to the top in one complete revolution. As the wheel rotates, the plow digs into the soil, making space for the seeds to sink in, root down, and rise up:

Rest & Rise Cycle

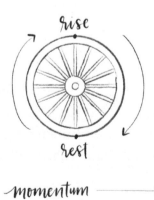

rise

rest

momentum ⟶

Notice that the turning wheel does not stay in one place. When attached to the plow powered by the beasts of burden, its movement creates forward momentum.

As we rest and rise, as we take Jesus' yoke and let Him bear the bulk of our burden. We move forward in God's purpose for us. This purpose is spelled out in the Great Commission:

"And Jesus came and said to them, 'All authority in heaven and on earth has been given to me. Go therefore and make disciples of all nations, baptizing them in the name of the Father and of the Son and of the Holy Spirit, teaching them to observe all that I have commanded you. And behold, I am with you always, to the end of the age.'"—Matthew 28:18-20

Jesus' last commandment is our first priority and main purpose: to make disciples. Making disciples is the work and His people are the harvest. As Jesus taught Peter and Andrew how to fish for men, our purpose is to raise up others in the Lord. As you *Rise*, you will receive suggestions and exercises to help you live this out and love others.

RALLY

It's easy to feel that the regular cycle of seasons is madness on a merry-go-round—the stars fade, the sun appears. We sleep, wake, work, watch cat videos, and start over. As we do work on our own, let us not get stuck into thinking we are alone in the work. Let us *Rally* together and share what God has been doing.

One person's work may be connected a single wheel, but when we zoom out, we can see the bigger picture. The wheel is connected to the plow. Step back further, and the whole field comes into view. We're not the only ones out there laboring. People working on their own sections of the field dot the quilted landscape and suddenly, we feel as if we are part of a bigger plan.

We have three days of individual work with the Lord, and then we gather together and share what the Lord has been doing in our field. When we *Rally*, we see the bigger picture, learn more about who God is through the rest and work cycles of others, and bond through shared experiences. It is a time of merriment, enjoying the fruits of our labor and going deeper with one another.

You will find a recipe to share, a prayer to rest, and a question to break the ice. You may spend time reflecting on your past week's study, and end with a *Rally* cry to close the time.

RECAP

Recapping the week is one way to solidify the message in our minds. Wrapping up gives us an accountability challenge for real life application, and is an opportunity to share our heart with others. This part is best done the day after meeting with your group or the last day of your individual study.

WEEK ONE

Come to Jesus

(Matthew 11:28)

DAY ONE

"Come to me, all who labor and are heavy laden, and I will give you rest." - Matthew 11:28

"Come to me, and I'll give you rest," the TV seems to call from the middle of the living room, while the comfy couch joins the chorus, and I suddenly remember my aching feet.

"I have worked really hard today. I do deserve to relax," I respond in my mind and plop down to watch a show with my husband.

But I can't just sit down and do nothing, because according to my personal productivity framework, that would be lazy. So I do the hard work of getting out the step ladder and reaching back to the far recesses of the pantry where I hid the candy corn. "I should at least work on making this candy bag go away so I'll stop thinking about it," I reason. Now I'm doing something industrious while resting at the same time. I'm pretty pleased with my compromise.

After I eat too much candy corn, fold laundry, and practice hand lettering, the show is over and I'm too tired to make a move. So I choose the next best constructive task and check my email. I drag myself to bed, but I can't sleep because I've had too much blue light exposure and sugar, and am past the point of tiredness.

Sigh.

This is not rest.

Jesus knows I need it.

He knows we all need real rest, not to "veg-out" and pass out (which has nothing to do with consuming nourishing vegetables).

But how can how can we sit down when we know we have things to do, people to see, and places to go?

But how can we sleep when we have notifications popping up on our phone, reminding us that we have responsibilities requiring our attention?

But how can we rest when our dreams aren't fulfilled? How can we see those dreams come to fruition when the realities of life and necessity to sleep keeps getting in the way?

There are plenty of things in life that offer rest: gentle music, candles, lavender, a warm bed, a cozy blanket, a hot beverage. While these are all good gifts, Jesus invites us to come directly to the gift giver.

REST

Assume a position of humility. That can be knees bowed, head low, palms turned upward, face up to the sky, whatever posture waves the white flag before the Lord and communicates, "I surrender!"

Fill in the prayer below:

Jesus,
Thank you for _____.

You are my _____ (i.e. Resting Place, Friend, Healer).

I give up my cares and plans to You today:

_____

_____

_____

Set a timer for one minute. Breathe deeply and release every muscle, starting from your toes and working up to your forehead. When your mind starts to wander like an ox for greener pastures, repeat Jesus's words, "Come to me."

For video instruction, head to
kaseybshuler.com/shop/restandrisestudy.

Let me rest my worth in your finished work. Let this offering of silence be pleasing to you, O Lord, my rock and my redeemer. Amen!

REFLECT

*"**Come to me**, all who labor and are heavy laden, and I will give you rest." Matthew 11:28*

Write the verse below:

_____

_____

_____

"Come to me"

How do you picture Jesus when He is extending this invitation?

Rest is typically thought of as "ceasing from activity." Think about the word "come." Is this word passive or active?

How does your answer change your definition of engaging in the rest of Jesus?

'Rest!' the rabbi exclaims, spit spraying from his mouth as it does when he's excited. 'But not only! Because menucha doesn't simply mean a pause from work. A break from exertion. It isn't just the opposite of toil and labor. If it took a special act of creation to bring it into being, surely it must be something extraordinary. Not the negative of something that already existed, but a unique positive, without which the universe would be incomplete. No, not just rest,' the rabbi says. 'Tranquility! Serenity! Repose! Peace.'[5]

I've heard it said, "the answer is always 'no' until you ask." Can you think of any instances in the Bible when those who came to Jesus did not find the rest and healing they needed?

What did the following people have to overcome to approach Jesus? How did Jesus receive each of them?

Luke 5:19

---

[5] Nicole Krauss, Forest Dark (New York, Harper Collins, 2017).

Luke 17:12-13

Luke 18:15-16

What obstacles do you need to overcome to find rest today?

Think about a stressful or sorrowful moment. What was your first reaction? Where or to whom do you turn?

What are the best ways to find rest in the following? You may fill in the blanks with your personal preferences. I've completed the first two for you:

TV   *watch*
Couch   *sit*
Hot cocoa
Book
Hammock
_____

_____

_____

Jesus

How did you answer the last one? Going to Jesus for rest is freeing because there is no one way to do it. He made us all differently and meets us in our place of rest. For some, that can be knitting indoors. For others, it might be hiking in nature. With Jesus, you're free to be you!

When the Israelites sought rest in Jeremiah 31:2-3, where did the Lord appear?

Where was He leading them (see Jeremiah 31:12)?

When you need rest, you may simply pray, "I'm here." Look and listen to where He wants to lead you.

RISE

I encourage you to find a space to be with Jesus this week. Write down that place or activity where you will meet Him when you need rest.

Read Psalm 115:4-8. Think about what you worship in your need for rest, and write a prayer to God asking to become more like Jesus:

Record anything else that comes to mind (a poem, a thought, or drawing):

What is one thing the Lord has given you today that you can generously share with someone else? It can be words of wisdom, a compassionate hug, an item of need or act of service.

As you rise to your feet, invite the Spirit to rise within you.

DAY TWO

"Come to me, all who labor and are heavy laden, and I will give you rest." Matthew 11:28

REST

Sink into a restful position of surrender before the Lord.

Fill in the prayer below:

Jesus,
Thank you for _____.

You are my _____ (i.e. Deliverer, Anchor, Reward).

I give up my cares and plans to You today:

_____

_____

_____

Set a timer for two minutes. Breathe deeply and release every muscle, starting from your toes and working up to your forehead. When your mind starts to wander like an ox for greener pastures, repeat Jesus's words, "Come to me, all who labor and are heavy laden."

Let me rest my worth in your finished work. Let this offering of silence be pleasing to you, O Lord, my rock and my redeemer. Amen!

REFLECT

"Come to me, **all who labor and are heavy laden**, and I will give you rest." Matthew 11:28

Write the verse below:

_____

_____

_____

"...all who labor and are heavy laden..."

Our church congregation always sings when prompted by the worship team on stage, but this time, I knew we sang with our whole hearts. We cried out,

A thrill of hope

The weary world rejoices

For yonder breaks

A new and glorious morn!

Getting ourselves into the room on Sunday morning was a struggle in itself. Looking around the room and knowing a handful of personal stories, I acknowledge their battle and give thanks for their presence. A college student showed up and took a break from studying for finals. A mom is on time with all of her five kids--and they all have their clothes on and hair brushed. A husband sings next to his wife, even though they are in the middle of an unresolved argument. An older gentleman puts his arm around his grandchildren. I know he must be in pain and it would be easier to sleep in and stay in bed. But still, he stands and sings.

We are the weary world.

Using Webster's Dictionary 1828 - Online Edition[6], look up the word "labor" and write down the definition that best describes how you understand labor.

Read Genesis 1. What was work like in the beginning?

---

[6] www.webstersdictionary1828.com

In the beginning, God spoke and it was so. His Word and will are one—what He speaks, He accomplishes. He said, "let there be grass," and green blades sprang into being. No thorns, no pain, no manipulation involved. As human beings made in His image, I imagine that's how work was meant to be for Adam and Eve. Whatever they put their mind to, their hands could create!

Nothing got in the way and everything continued as it should, until death entered through sin and became the great obstacle to good work. God breathed life into man, and man inhaled and exhaled in an unceasing cycle...until death interrupted. Man's breath fell, as did the shovel from his hand. God's work is meant to be unceasing and without obstacles—unbroken and steadfast—just as His love is for us.

Read Genesis 3:16-19. What words now describe work?

For Eve:

For Adam:

Instead of creating life, work for Adam and Eve created problems. Adam and Eve wanted to do well, but found that after the fall, they constantly fell short.

This is the nature of labor mentioned in Matthew 11:28. The word "labor" Jesus uses refers to the effort that the Israelites expended to keep up with the Pharisaic law. God gave one rule to Adam and Eve and ten rules to the Israelites in the wilderness. These were good boundaries to keep them safe from the destructive effects of sin. But by the time Jesus arrived on the scene, the religious leaders had added over 600 addendums. These rules did not help people sin less; as the rules increased, so did opportunities to fail.

Look back at the definition of the word "labor." The root of it means "to fail." It's as if failure is built into labor. Good intentions are not enough for the righteousness we seek. Even when we try to get it right, we eventually meet failure in some form. Another law is put into place, the bar gets higher and even more impossible to reach. Instead of helping us progress forward, this circuit of futility leads us straight to a dead end wall (refer to the "Rest and Rise Cycle" in *Overview* for the answer to this dilemma).

Take a moment to read Ecclesiastes 2:11. Do you ever feel the vanity of your efforts? If so, explain.

Do you feel like you have ever failed? Describe a specific instance.

Would you consider yourself to be one who labors? What is your greatest source of labor?

Define heavy laden using Isaiah 1:4 and Psalm 38:3-8.

Isaiah 1:4:

Psalm 38:3-8:

How does Psalm 38:3-6 relate physical health to the burden of sin?

When I think of heavy burdens I picture someone carrying around a bulging pack. Most jobs in the internet age require staring at a screen. And for those of us who spend time looking down at an electronic device, this is how our body looks—shoulders slumping downwards and head jutting forward, like we have an invisible burden on our back.

What do you spend most of your time looking at or working on? How has it shaped your body, your thoughts, and your actions?

Body:

Thoughts:

Actions:

I work as a personal trainer in the fitness industry, I see messages like "no pain, no gain" and "no excuses" being used to get people moving and motivated. Messages of shame don't move us forward, they weigh us down.

Voices like these act like the Egyptian taskmasters who forced the Israelites to build bricks without straw. These taskmasters are like a mirror saying, "You have wrinkles," without the power to help you turn back time, or a scale saying you're overweight without helping you lose the pounds.

What taskmasters or messages weigh you down with no intention of building you up? You can usually find these in your places of work and responsibility.

The student wants to pass the test, the waitress wants to go home with a pocketful of tips, and the salesman wants to make commission. We want to succeed with what we have been given, but the desires of the flesh threaten to pull us away from our good intentions. A girl distracts the student, the waitress lingers in the back to gossip about a rude patron, and the salesman breaches company conduct to make an extra buck.

Likewise, God has placed an internal knowledge of Himself within each of us. So no one is without excuse (see Romans 1:19-21). We may know what is right, but we don't have the ability to carry it out on our own. We work to reap rewards, but we often feel heavy laden from our efforts. We become conflicted within, finding no rest.

See Romans 7:18-25. What was Paul's solution to the passions warring within him (see verse 25)?

Author Elise Fitzpatrick says this about the gospel: "no fluff, no bricks, only good news."[7] The gospel of Christ isn't a vain pursuit full of hot air, nor is it a pile of bricks you have to carry around. Yes, the gospel shows us our sin, and that's hard to handle. But Jesus does the heavy lifting, empowering you to rise up. He has won the war, and empowers you to win daily battles with temptation.

RISE

Let's take a moment and realign our spines. Try standing against a wall. Think of the wall as your plumb line, like Jesus to our righteousness. Stand with the back of your head against the wall, place heels six inches from the wall. Your lumbar curve and shoulder blades should touch the wall. There should be less than 2 inches between your neck or small of the back and the wall. Keeping that posture, walk away from the wall. Go back to this exercise when you feel like the demands of your day are pulling you down.

Even when we have been freed from sin through the cross of Christ, our taskmasters (i.e. shame over past sins, spirits of anxiety and doubt) can still pursue us, just as the Egyptians chased the Israelites after they had been freed from slavery. Write out a prayer to the Lord using Exodus 15:4-6 as a template, trusting He will come through for you:

---

[7] Elyse Fitzpatrick, "No Fluff, No Bricks, Just Good News," *Elyse Fitzpatrick*, https://www.elysefitzpatrick.com.

Record anything else that comes to mind (a poem, a thought, a drawing):

What is one thing the Lord has given you today that you will share with someone else? It can be wisdom in the form of words, compassion in the form of a hug, service in the form of meeting someone's need.

As you rise to your feet, invite the Spirit to rise within you.

DAY THREE

"Come to me, all who labor and are heavy laden, and I will give you rest." Matthew 11:28

REST

Find a prayerful position, and fill in the prayer below:

Jesus,

Thank you for _____.

You are my _____ (i.e. Resurrection, Security, Salvation).

I give up my cares and plans to You today:

_____

_____

_____

Set a timer for three minutes. Breathe deeply and release every muscle, starting from your toes and working up to your forehead. When your mind starts to wander like an ox for greener pastures, repeat Jesus's words, "Come to me, all who labor and are heavy laden, and I will give you rest."

Let me rest my worth in your finished work. Let this offering of silence be pleasing to you, O Lord, my rock and my redeemer. Amen!

REFLECT

*"Come to me, all who labor and are heavy laden, **and I will give you rest.**" Matthew 11:28*

Write the verse below:

_____

_____

_____

"...I will give you rest."

Restful activities are all useful, but do they fill our soul with the rest we truly desire? External activities are limited by the world they exist to serve, but God has no limits. Jesus exposes this problem of trying to find rest in the world and volunteers Himself as the solution. These words come out of the same mouth that spoke Lazarus into life. The grave isn't the only thing that can give us rest—Jesus has the power to give us rest right now.

Think about the things in your life that have promised rest. Have any of them let you down or disappointed you?

Write down Numbers 23:19:

How does this give you reassurance that God can and will provide rest?

Carl Bloch depicted Jesus inviting all who labor and are heavy laden to come to Him in his painting, *Christ the Consoler*. If you can, look it up and write down who you are in the audience.

Are you the guy clinging to Jesus' robes or the child on the sidelines looking for a way out?

When I'm feeling desperate, I'm on the right side, in my happy place with Jesus. When I'm on my own path, I'm the impatient character thinking, "How much longer until this sermon is over? I have a to-do list to tackle so I can go to sleep before midnight." But physical rest does not guarantee soul rest. Rest requires both body and soul to experience rest for true peace, for *shalom*. Shalom is complete peace, a gift from God, and is a common farewell among the Jewish people. We often say, "take care," as a way to bless the person with what we think they are looking for. *Shalom* is a more full expression of our hope for rest.

Skim the "hall of faith" in Hebrews 11. Using Hebrews 11:39 as a reference, did these faithful men and women receive *shalom*?

If faith is defined as what we hope for but have not yet obtained, what is the point of our faith? See 1 Peter 1:9.

Fill in the blanks in 1 Thessalonians 5:23-24 below:

"Now may the God of peace himself sanctify you completely, and may your whole _____ and _____ and _____ be kept blameless at the coming of our Lord Jesus Christ. He who calls you is faithful; he will surely do it."

What does the phrase "he will surely do it" mean for you today?

RISE

What will you do when you need rest—emotionally, mentally, physically, and spiritually?

Write a personal prayer for the day incorporating Colossians 3:1:

Record anything else that comes to mind (a poem, a thought, a drawing):

What is one thing the Lord has given you today that you will share with someone else? It can be wisdom in the form of words, compassion in the form of a hug, or service in the form of meeting someone's need.

As you rise to your feet, invite the Spirit to rise within you.

RALLY

Recipe
Caprese Salad On A Stick, makes 30

This recipe may have a fancy name, but it's incredibly easy to prep. Skip the salami for the vegetarians in your life, and proudly serve this dish to the hungry masses...or a crowd of 30.

Ingredients:

- 1 Carton grape tomatoes (at least 30 count)
- 30 Fresh mozzarella cheese balls
- 30 Slices of salami
- 30 Fresh medium-sized basil leaves
- 1 Cup balsamic vinegar
- Toothpicks

Directions:

In a saucepan over high heat, bring balsamic vinegar to a boil. As soon as it starts boiling, lower heat to medium and simmer for ten minutes or until thickened enough to coat the back of a spoon. Remove from heat to let cool. Assemble the toothpicks by skewering one tomato, one basil leaf, one folded slice of salami, and one mozzarella ball.

You could also start with one end of the basil leaf, a tomato, a mozzarella ball, and then wrap the other end of the leaf around the end. Assemble on a plate and drizzle with balsamic reduction. Serve chilled and enjoy!

PRAYER

Spend a moment in silence listening for the Lord to speak a different word to you or say this prayer:

"Lord, we thank you that you do not demand that we come to you, but you invite us. You know our hearts. You know that we are tired and worn out people. You know exactly what we need, and you meet us where we are. God, you are so good! We thank you for loving us and we surrender our preconceived notions of rest and work, we surrender our need to fill the silence, we surrender our fear of saying the wrong thing. You are with us, and with you is all the victory. Amen."

Icebreaker question: Would you rather watch TV for 12 hours or hike for 12 hours?

Share your story: What is your history with rest and work? Why did you decide to do this study?

What stuck out during this week's study? What does it say about you and about God, and how can you apply it?

When we need rest, we first go to Jesus. *Are you an extrovert or introvert? How can we serve one another when we "labor and are heavy laden"?*

Ending benediction. Make a huddle while holding hands, then say this prayer:

"Jesus, may we find rest in You and rise with purpose. Amen!"

 Lift each others' arms up at the end.

RECAP

Memory verse: "Come to me, all who labor and are heavy laden, and I will give you rest." Matthew 11:28

Message: Come to Jesus.

Social Media Challenge: The next time you are in your "Rest and Rise" spot or activity with the Lord, snap a picture and share it on social media, asking others to share theirs with #restandrisestudy. Take note of the different ways people find rest in the Lord. Praise God for the variety of ways we can come to Him.

WEEK TWO

Take His Yoke

(Matthew 11:29a)

DAY ONE

"Take my yoke upon you, and learn from me..."
Matthew 11:29a

During our church Community Group, the leader posed the question, "How do we rest in a productivity-centered society?" We went around and gave our answers based on life experience and Scripture. Then came the prayer requests. One father of five talked about the pressures of his work and how he felt like he needed to conform to the intense attitude of his new cohort. He was relaxed in nature, but did not want his calm demeanor to be seen as incompetence. At home, he found himself yearning to disciple his family as he quickly blew leaves off the porch like a good homeowner.

I absolutely feel his pain. How can we be fully ourselves while abiding by the set standards of our work atmosphere? How do we obey God's exalted work of discipling while also meeting the demands of everyday life on the ground? In short, how can we do God's pure and holy work in a broken and complex world?

For me, this question is completely overwhelming. And as a five on the Enneagram[8], I tend to ball up and shut down, like an armadillo at the sound of an incoming threat. But I know that after I come out of hiding, the problem is still there, staring me in the face with a big dumb grin. I find Jesus' invitation to take His yoke oddly peace-giving.

Jesus did not remain in the Highest Heaven, secluded within the Holy place, surrounded by legions of worshipping angels. He came down to an unsuspecting, unwelcoming world. Jesus tore the veil between the heaven and earth to help us figure out how to be both human and holy.

While we focus on keeping our exterior lives compartmentalized and tidy, God cares more about a clean heart washed by His Word and prayer: "For everything created by God is good, and nothing is to be rejected if it is received with thanksgiving, for it is made holy by the word of God and prayer" (1 Timothy 4:4-5). When we partner our thoughts in prayer with His written Word, we invite the Spirit to touch our lives and make it holy (see Isaiah 6:5-7). He can transform a simple chore like leaf blowing into an act of discipleship.

But as much as we try, we will get distracted by what we see and lose sight of the Lord. The Holy Spirit helps us in our weaknesses, and God still honors the father of five and his desires to serve the family with a clean yard, to lead his children, and to excel in the workplace, even if he does miss a leaf or two.

We don't have to do everything right, because we have Jesus as our perfect leader. He takes responsibility for those He serves. When we come to the end of our abilities and take Jesus up on

---

[8] For more information on the Enneagram Profiles and tests, check out: https://www.enneagraminstitute.com

His offer of partnership, He takes on the burden of success and failure in our work and relationships. When we know we can't, He can. It's not all up to us anymore.

When His yoke is on, the pressure comes off! We are free to try hard and fail big because the outcome is not our responsibility. Jesus has already secured the outcome, and He wins. And because we share His yoke, we win too. May this grace empower us to lean on Jesus' strength as we pull the yoke side-by-side.

REST

Find a prayerful position, and fill in the prayer below:

Jesus,
Thank you for _____.

You are my _____ (i.e. Redeemer, Lord, Helper).

I give up my cares and plans to You today:

_____

_____

_____

Set a timer for four minutes. Breathe deeply and release every muscle, starting from your toes and working up to your forehead. When your mind starts to wander like an ox for greener pastures, repeat Jesus's words, "Take my yoke."

Let me rest my worth in your finished work. Let this offering of silence be pleasing to you, O Lord, my rock and my redeemer. Amen!

REFLECT

*"Come to me, all who labor and are heavy laden, and I will give you rest. **Take my yoke upon you**, and learn from me..."* Matthew 11:28-29a

Write the verse below:

_____

_____

_____

"Take my yoke upon you..."

Since the only yolks we usually come into contact with are the ones on the breakfast table, let's talk about yolk's homonym, yoke. The word *yoke* refers to the crossbar that hooks two beasts of burden together for work, such as plowing a field (see above picture).

Previously in the Bible, the word was used to refer to the heavy yoke of the law. But God is our Redeemer. He redeems the word *yoke* and turns it into an opportunity to work with Him, building our relationship and the Kingdom.

Today, we will cover two characteristics of a yoke: submission and restraint. These aren't always pleasant words, but the Lord's yoke is light and easy. Let's stick together in letting God redefine them.

Why do we even need a yoke in the first place? Why can't we just do the work by ourselves? Read the following passages and describe what each person needs and why:

Genesis 2:18

Exodus 18:18-23

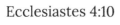

Ecclesiastes 4:10

What do you need help with today, and why?

In order to be fitted with a yoke, we must bow our head and receive the bar on our necks. Whether we realize it or not, we already wear a yoke—but it may not be the gentle yoke of Christ. What do we submit ourselves to throughout the course of a day? This is anything we feel like we "need" or "should" do. Is this activity life-giving or depleting (2 Corinthians 3:6)?

Not all yokes are obvious or self-imposed. For example, we all face the restraint of social constructs. Author Brené Brown outlines the general expectations for women: "If women want to play by the rules, they need to be sweet, thin, and pretty, stay quiet, be perfect moms and wives, and not own their power."[9] Below, write down the boundaries you abide by according to your current season of life, and describe if it makes you feel more alive or deadens your spirit:

Vocational responsibilities	Life Giving or Depleting
-	
-	
Family duties	
-	
-	
Social obligations	
-	
-	
Other	
-	
-	

---

[9] Brené Brown, *Daring Greatly: How the Courage to Be Vulnerable Transforms the Way We Live, Love, Parent, and Lead* (New York: Avery Publication, 2015), 107.

Responsibilities, duties, and obligations are all variations of human law. What or who does God tell us to submit to?

James 4:7

Hebrews 13:17

Romans 13:1

Ephesians 5:22-25

What does God's Word tell us not to submit to?

Galatians 5:1

Based on your answers above, is there a burdensome yoke you want to break free from to gladly accept the burden-lifting yoke of Christ?

Unlike the lofty CEO or ruling tyrant, God doesn't order us to do His grunt work .

Jesus went first. He is the One who lowers Himself under the yoke. Jesus shows us a servant God by bending low and washing the feet of His bewildered disciples. His whole life is an example of what it is like to submit to God in joyful reverence, to be perfected through suffering, and finally, exalted in glory.

What else did Jesus submit himself to?

Matthew 4:1

Philippians 2:8

For some practical examples of biblical restraint, see Proverbs 17:27, 2 Corinthians 12:7, and 1 Corinthians 9:25.

The Pharisees and religious teachers of Jesus' day had an appearance of practicing restraint through their stringent observance of the Sabbath, fasting, and tithing down to the tenth herb leaf. This is not godly self-control, it's a futile attempt at self-righteousness through man-made regulations. If I go on a strict diet that tells me exactly what to eat, I can say "no" to junk food more easily than when I'm not on a program. But a program is only temporary, and the gospel is eternal. God has His eyes set on a steadfast solution for our body, mind, and spirit. Colossians 2:20-23 says this about regulations:

If with Christ you died to the elemental spirits of the world, why, as if you were still alive in the world, do you submit to regulations— "Do not handle, Do not taste, Do not touch" (referring to things that all perish as they are used)—according to human precepts and teachings? These have indeed an appearance of wisdom in promoting self-made religion and asceticism and severity to the body, but they are of no value in stopping the indulgence of the flesh.

Where do you rely on systems instead of the Spirit?

While Jesus did practice restraint in holding back His command of the army of angels (see Matthew 26:53), He also practices restraint in forcing people to obey God. The Pharisees, however, frequently demanded that Jesus throw the first stone[10], dictate the Sabbath rules[11], and keep social order by separating from those who were considered unclean[12].

In John 8:3-6, Mark 3:1-4, and Luke 7:39, what were the motives of the Pharisees?

How do Jesus' responses give us freedom to follow Him?

What does John 3:17 say about who God is and what He desires for us?

---

[10] John 8:3-6
[11] Mark 3:1-4
[12] Luke 7:39

God restrains His wrath to unleash His mercy. For more examples of this, see Isaiah 48:9, Psalm 104:9, and Daniel 6:22.

In 1 Thessalonians 4:1-2, does Paul demand the church to obey God? How does he position himself in his request to them, and what does this say about our attitude towards others?

RISE

When I wear jeans that fit too snug, my breathing is restricted and I feel irritable. Hebrews 12:1 says, "let us also lay aside every weight, and sin which clings so closely, and let us run with endurance the race that is set before us." Let us practice peeling away oppressing sin in exchange for an unhindered pursuit of the Lord. In response, take out one piece of clothing in your closet that feels constricting and distracting, and set it aside to give away.

Write a personal prayer for the day here, incorporating Psalm 40:11 into your prayer of thanksgiving.

Record anything else that comes to mind (a poem, a thought, a drawing):

What is one thing the Lord has given you today that you will share with someone else? It can be wisdom in the form of words, compassion in the form of a hug, service in the form of meeting someone's need.

As you rise to your feet, invite the Spirit to rise within you.

DAY TWO

REST

Find a prayerful position, and fill in the prayer below:

Jesus,
Thank you for _____.

You are my _____ (i.e. King, Leader, Partner).

I give up my cares and plans to You today:

_____

_____

_____

Set a timer for five minutes. Breathe deeply and release every muscle, starting from your toes and working up to your forehead. When your mind starts to wander like an ox for greener pastures, repeat Jesus's words, "Take my yoke upon you, and learn from me."

Let me rest my worth in your finished work. Let this offering of silence be pleasing to you, O Lord, my rock and my redeemer. Amen!

REFLECT

*"Come to me, all who labor and are heavy laden, and I will give you rest. **Take my yoke upon you,** and learn from me..."* Matthew 11:28-29a

Write the verse below:

_____

_____

_____

"Take my yoke upon you..."

Yokes are attached to plows to till fields and ready the ground to receive seeds. Yokes are a tool, an integral part in producing a fruitful crop. But if we always keep our head down in the dirt, we lose sight of the bigger picture of our work.

In this myopic view, much of life can seem reactionary—there's an emergency at work and we need to put out a fire, there are emails to be read, dirt to be swept (and leaves to be blown). But when we rest and step back from our work and create distance, we can stop and ask ourselves the purpose of our work. Let's spend some proactive time focusing on the harvest. What do you want to accomplish with your work?

Who is your work for?

Why do you do it?

What is the result of your work?

What did Jesus want to accomplish with His work on earth? Read Luke 19:10 and write it below:

What is the work of God?

John 6:29

This doesn't seem productive according to worldly metrics. In the modern sense of the word, productivity equates to visible results. When this becomes our focus, people become valued for their output—numbers are gold and names are lost in the slush. This is a hard line to walk in organizations like nonprofits, who depend on their ability to show numbers of people reached to attract more donors. Even churches can get caught up in the numbers game. But I know from experience that a small, local church can have just as much impact as a mega church. Success is not a room full of people, but people filled with the Lord's rest.

What does God want us to do? Read John 15:16-17 and Matthew 11:28-30. Write them below in your own words.

John 15:16-17

Matthew 11:28-30

True or false: My work starts when I do.

Let us practice discernment and review the outcome of our labor. Yesterday, we established that we wear a yoke—we need help from our spouse, friends, and coworkers. We submit to our supervisors, government, and even to the culture around us. The question is not will we put on a yoke, but who do we partner with in our work?

Ephesians 5:7 exhorts us not to become partners with disobedience, but to walk with the Spirit. We can either walk with Jesus, or with the prince of disobedience. The Spirit is the yoke that connects us with Jesus, and the flesh is the yoke that connects us with the enemy.

Fill out the chart below with the work that you do during the day and what it produces within you using the lists from Galatians 5. Name the yoke that you were under, and lift a prayer of submission to the Spirit (whether in thanksgiving or supplication). Jesus can take our burden when we take His yoke. I did the first one as an example.

Works of the flesh: sexual immorality, impurity, sensuality, idolatry, sorcery, enmity, strife, jealousy, fits of anger, rivalries, dissensions, divisions, envy, drunkenness, orgies, and things like these

Fruit of the Spirit: love, joy, peace, patience, kindness, goodness, faithfulness, gentleness, self-control

Work	Produces	Yoke	Prayer
Parenting	fits of anger	flesh	Spirit, I need patience
	self-control	Spirit	Thank you Jesus!

Spiritual fruit is different from works of the flesh. Spiritual fruit is what we were made for; this harvest is our inheritance. The many works of the flesh divide our hearts and keep our wills under constant compulsion, driving us to do more and more. But we do not need to do more, we need what is right.

Our role as children of God is not to become systematic robots on the assembly line of production—it is to be fruitful and multiply (Genesis 9:7). This cultural mandate is not just for procreation. We are to be fruitful in every workplace, every vocation, and every place that God has used His voice to create an opportunity for us to work and reign as stewards over the earth. As evidenced in the variety of creation, He doesn't want us to create clones of ourselves, but to create new life after the image of our Creator God. As we reproduce goodness in our space, we spread the glory of the Lord until His fame fills the earth, as the waters cover the sea. Let us be fruitful and multiply!

RISE

When tensions rise today and you need help, think about what you will partner with in the moment: love or fear, freedom or punishment, Jesus or the enemy. No matter how many times we have partnered with the flesh, whenever we feel broken down in despair or despondent in heart, Jesus consistently returns to us, saying gently as a father offering a wounded child His hand, "Here, take my yoke." Take a risk on love and offer your hand to someone else today.

Write a personal prayer of thanksgiving for the day here, incorporating Psalm 118:5-7.

Record anything else that comes to mind (a poem, a thought, a drawing):

What is one thing the Lord has given you today that you will share with someone else? It can be wisdom in the form of words, compassion in the form of a hug, service in the form of meeting someone's need.

As you rise to your feet, invite the Spirit to rise within you.

DAY THREE

REST

Find a prayerful position, and fill in the prayer below:

Jesus,

Thank you for _____.

You are my _____ (i.e. Guide, Teacher, Master).

I give up my cares and plans to You today:

_____

_____

_____

Set a timer for six minutes. Breathe deeply and release every muscle, starting from your toes and working up to your forehead. When your mind starts to wander like an ox for greener pastures, repeat Jesus's words, "Take my yoke upon you, and learn from me."

Let me rest my worth in your finished work. Let this offering of silence be pleasing to you, O Lord, my rock and my redeemer. Amen!

REFLECT

*"Come to me, all who labor and are heavy laden, and I will give you rest. Take my yoke upon you, **and learn from me**..."* Matthew 11:28-29a

Write the verse below:

_____

_____

_____

"...and learn from me..."

Sometimes I envy the disciples. They had the unique privilege of being able to walk and talk with Jesus face-to-face, to eat the bread that Jesus multiplied, to stand in the boat when Jesus hushed the storm, to enjoy the wine from water. When I compare myself to another generation, I forget His blessings on ours: "Nevertheless, I tell you the truth: it is to your advantage that I go away, for if I do not go away, the Helper will not come to you. But if I go, I will send him to you" (John 16:7).

We have the Holy Spirit to teach our hearts. Jesus said this is better because His Spirit can move inside us and teach the innermost parts of our life, counseling us through every thought, word, and deed.

I witnessed what Jesus meant by this as I sat in the audience during my three-year-old's dance recital. At first, the dance teacher was out in front while toddlers tried their best to follow along behind her. In the proceeding performances, dancers grew older and the teacher moved backstage.

Eventually, she could not be seen at all. The teacher's instruction had moved from before the dancers' eyes to within their hearts. As the more experienced dancers leapt across the stage with trained grace, I saw the joy in their eyes as they lived out years of instruction and glorified their teacher.

This is what it is like to learn from Jesus, only His ways are even better. We are not confined to a classroom or a stage; our omnipresent God teaches us through every movement of daily life. The word "learn" in this passage is the Greek word *manthano*, the verb from which *mathetes*, "disciple," originates. A disciple of Jesus is one who learns from Him.

To learn is to listen. Listening is one of the most sacrificial acts of self-forgetfulness. And I don't mean the type of half-hearted listening where our eyes are on our phone and our mouth simply repeats what the person said. To listen and learn, we shut down selfishness and turn up humility. To lean in to another's teaching is to press pause on our own agenda to focus on theirs. Our discipline in solitude and silence at the end of each *Rise* section strengthens the part of our brain that is required for focus.

Distractions are a temptation, and can be resisted. But every time we chase that distraction we create a new pathway in our brain, fragmenting our neural communication system, like a divergent stream from a river. Practicing mindfulness, or attentive listening to the Lord, strengthens the river and the peace that flows from it.

There is even scientific evidence that increased mindfulness strengthens the integrity of the vagal nerve, the nerve that connects the brain and gut. Inflammation and anxiety decreases, and a sense of calm and ability to adapt to outside stressors increases.[13] This act of pure listening serves to heal us, pull our parts together, and make us whole.

Do you take time during your day to listen for the Lord? If so, when?

If not, think about the small spaces and margin in your life: sitting at a stop light, waiting in line, staring at the download bar, or before you close your eyes to sleep. Which of those moments could you use as a sanctuary in time to be still and listen, saying, "Speak, for your servant hears" (1 Samuel 3:10b)?

When is a time you felt like God was speaking or you heard that gentle voice guiding you, but you decided not to listen? Why? What was the outcome?

---

[13] Chris Kesser, "How Distraction is Rewiring our Brains—And How Mindfulness Can Help," *Kresser Institute for Functional and Evolutionary Medicine*, November 27, 2016, https://kresserinstitute.com/distraction-rewiring-brains-mindfulness-can-help.

I think of Martha running around the house and preparing for her guests, while the most important guest, Jesus, was sitting and waiting for her to come to Him. Submitting to Jesus' yoke of rest is a choice. He infrequently makes us slow down, stop, listen, and learn from Him. What did Mary choose, according to Luke 10:24?

What do you think Martha learned in this situation?

Even though she had good intentions, she was missing the point—the person of God in plain sight. He was there all along, sitting calmly at the center of her hurricane.

When we pull the burdens of life by the yoke of our own performance, then performance sets the pace. We race faster and faster, trying to outdo our last personal best or to measure up to the expectations of others. But when we take on the yoke of Christ and let Him lead, He determines the pace, and we find that His grace makes up what we are lacking in our performance. - Kerri Weems[14]

When I am yoked with performance, I go so fast I end up tearing up the field. When I am yoked with discontent, I stray completely to seek out other pastures.

---

[14] Kerri Weems, *Rhythms of Grace: Discovering God's Tempo For Your Life* (Grand Rapids: Zondervan, 2014).

Being yoked beside Jesus is like this story:

"There was an old farmer plowing with a team of oxen. As I saw this team I was somewhat amazed, for one was a huge ox and the other a very small bullock. That ox towered over the little bullock that was sharing the work with him. I was amazed and perplexed to see a farmer trying to plow with two such unequal animals in the yoke and commented on the inequality to the man with whom I was riding. He stopped his car and said, 'I want you to notice something. See the way those traces are hooked to the yoke? You will observe that the large ox is pulling all the weight. That little bullock is being broken into the yoke but he is not actually pulling any weight.'"[15]

The yoke keeps us close to Him so we can learn from Him without actually pulling the weight of the burden.

Who is the person that God teaches?

Psalm 25:9

Where does He lead us, and what does He do for us?

Psalm 23:2-3

---

[15] Dwight Pentecost, *Design for Discipleship* (Grand Rapids, MI: Zondervan, 1971) 27-28.

RISE

To learn is to practice habitually. I would like you to try something with me. Let's move our bodies to the floor, then return to standing. Repeat three times. Pay attention to how your body feels.

How did it feel? How do you feel afterwards?

For me, it felt hard to get on the ground, but I felt energized afterwards. As we listen to the signals of our body through physical touch, may we listen to the Lord through His Word to our hearts. Psalm 116:7 tells us when we practice obedience by continually returning to the Lord for our rest, we will find abundant provision.

Referring to Proverbs 15:31, ask God for a humble heart to listen to correction and a brave spirit to do it.

Record anything else that comes to mind (a poem, a thought, a drawing):

What is one thing the Lord has taught you today that you will share with someone else? It can be wisdom in the form of words, compassion in the form of a hug, service in the form of meeting someone's need.

As you rise to your feet, invite the Spirit to rise within you.

RALLY

Recipe
Secret Ingredient Chocolate Truffles, makes 55

Keep the secret ingredient under wraps until *after* your friends eat these. For those who are allergic to anything healthy, they won't care about the black beans once they take a bite of these delicious morsels!

Ingredients:

- 1 can (15 ounces) black beans, rinsed and drained
- ⅓ cup chocolate chips of choice
- 1 ⅓ cups pitted medjool dates
- 1 Tablespoon + 1 teaspoon melted coconut oil, divided
- ½ cup + 2 teaspoons dark chocolate baking cocoa, divided
- 1 teaspoon vanilla extract
- 1/8 teaspoon salt

Directions:

Place the beans, chocolate chips, dates, 1 tablespoon coconut oil, ½ cup cocoa powder, vanilla, and salt in a food processor and process until blended. If the mixture is too thick, add a tablespoon of water at a time until it all comes together. You may need to stop and scrape down the sides once or twice. This could take a few minutes. Transfer the mixture into the fridge for 20 minutes to firm up. Refrigerate for at least twenty minutes to make the mixture firm. Place the remaining 2 teaspoons cocoa powder in a separate bowl. Rub a teaspoon of coconut oil into hands to prevent sticking, and roll a teaspoon-sized ball. Roll the truffle in the cocoa powder, then transfer to cookie sheet lined with parchment paper. Repeat with the remaining fudge mixture. Store in fridge until ready to serve. Enjoy!

Prayer

Spend a moment in silence listening for the Lord to speak a different word to you, or say this prayer:

"Jesus, thank you for offering Your yoke. It is so much better than our own ways. When we are hard-headed, help us to remember that Your yoke means restoration. Remind us that when we take Your yoke, You carry our burdens and we get to share in the joy of Your fruitfulness. Help us put ourselves aside in humility to truly listen to one another. We know that You hear each one of us. In your strong name we pray, amen."

Icebreaker question: Would you rather spend the next 24 hours alone or with a house full of guests?

Share your story: What is your definition of productivity and success? How do you think God measures a successful day?

What stuck out during this week's study? What does it say about you and about God, and how can you apply it?

We all need help. Let us partner with Jesus and learn His ways. Do you lean more towards independence or codependency? Under the care of Jesus, how can we move towards interdependence with each other?

Ending benediction. Say this prayer together with each person's right hand on the next person's shoulder, connected in a yoke of friendship:

"Jesus, may we find rest in You and rise with purpose. Amen!"

RECAP

Memory verse: "Take my yoke upon you, and learn from me..." Matthew 11:29a

Message: Let us turn from our own ways and partner with Jesus.

Social Media Challenge: Take a selfie of you and someone in your life who has helped you. In the caption, share a story of how that person has lifted your burdens as in Galatians 6:2: "Bear one another's burdens, and so fulfill the law of Christ." Below your story, challenge others to share a picture of them and their "helper" with #restandrisestudy. Celebrate how the Lord helps and lifts us up through others.

WEEK THREE

The Rest Our Soul Craves

(Matthew 11:29b)

DAY ONE

Have you ever had a friend, family member, or even a complete stranger bring you back onto emotional solid ground? You may have been feeling helpless and worthless, tossed about in the merciless ocean of life, or like a balloon snipped from the string, floating higher above the ground and losing control of your time and productivity.

A few weeks ago I was in need of some counsel. I knew beyond a shadow of a doubt the Lord had called me to start a faith and fitness ministry in my city through Revelation Wellness[16]. I had already conducted an 8-week faith and fitness program with a group of women and witnessed transformation in their lives. But when only one person showed up week after week in the fitness class, I started to wonder if this was the right fit for me. My personal training business was flourishing, the program went well, so why did I need to start a class in addition to my other offerings?

Whenever I brought my concerns to to the Lord in prayer, asking Him if I could let it fizzle out and gather more personal training clients instead, I felt a strong but gentle conviction that the answer was, "No." As hard as that was, I didn't quit. How could God's hand of blessing be on something so seemingly unfruitful? Aren't numbers and accolades a sign of success? If I couldn't weasel out of the battle, I would find a companion on the front lines. I sought out the help of Caroline, a local faith and fitness business owner.

---

[16]http://www.Revelationwellness.org

She graciously took some time out of her busy schedule (because her business was busy—the way I thought a busy-ness is supposed to work) to meet with me. After all the people lingering from the last class had gone, she sat down with me in a comfy chair adjacent to mine. She leaned in towards me and with that deeply penetrating gaze that melts your insides, asked me as genuinely as Jesus Himself would have asked, "Now, tell me what's on your heart." The look itself broke me a little bit, but when she asked, "Tell me what's on your heart?" and not "Tell me what's on your mind?" the walls fell and my eyes welled up from the overflow. She knew I was not there for Ten Tips on Running a Successful Business. I needed support and encouragement and she invited me to pour it all out.

When she asked me what questions I had for her, I felt the peace of the Lord settle me and give me what I came for, which was an undeniable sense of peace. And with that inner rest, a passion to keep going.

But I still wanted to know how she did it all, how she managed to meld the dust of the earth with the duties of God: "How do you balance family and work, while taking the time to create community and disciple others?" She admits she feels torn at times—when she is at home she feels the pull to go to work, and when she is at work she misses her family. But she exhorted me that to be all there, wherever I am. She told me to remember that whatever I do, do it for the Lord and not for other people.

That's what rest is all about. We find rest in Jesus, who is gentle and lowly in heart. There, we will find rest for our souls.

REST

Find a prayerful position, and fill in the prayer below:

Jesus,
Thank you for _____.

You are my _____ (i.e. Good Word, Lamb, Friend).

I give up my cares and plans to You today:

_____

_____

_____

Set a timer for seven minutes. Breathe deeply and release every muscle, starting from your toes and working up to your forehead. When your mind starts to wander like an ox for greener pastures, repeat Jesus's words, "for I am gentle and lowly in heart."

Let me rest my worth in your finished work. Let this offering of silence be pleasing to you, O Lord, my rock and my redeemer. Amen!

REFLECT

*"Come to me, all who labor and are heavy laden, and I will give you rest. Take my yoke upon you, and learn from me, **for I am gentle and lowly in heart**, and you will find rest for your souls."* Matthew 11:28-29

Write the verse below:

_____

_____

_____

_____

"...for I am gentle and lowly in heart..."

Name someone in your life who has exhibited a gentle spirit:

How did being with them make you feel?

According to 1 Peter 3:4, what is of great worth in God's sight?

The word "gentle" in the Greek means *meek*, which is strength under control, or the ability to restrain one's strength. In 1 Peter 3:4, the "gentle and quiet spirit" does not mean that women should refrain from speaking up; it refers to a settled, secure heart. A person exuding a gentle and quiet spirit is more impactful than any amount of flashy diamonds or impressive designer wear.

The word "gentle" is not only reserved for wives—gentleness characterizes strong men. I recall a mom at a playground admonishing her three-year-old boy to be gentle as he whacked a pole with a stick a foot away from another kid's face. I have had similar conversations with my own daughter, but instead of a flying stick it's a Cinderella crown. Trying to reassure the playground mom that gentleness took time to develop, I said, "Gentleness is strength under control. It takes time to train the gentleness muscle." Her eyes lit up and she asked her son, "Do you think you can be strong enough to be gentle?"

What is the opposite of gentle? Think of a time you have displayed this. What were the circumstances that brought it about, and how did it make you and others feel?

Circumstances:

How did it make you feel:

How did others feel:

Talk to the Lord about these circumstances. If you have not already, use this space to express your godly sorrow for grieving His Spirit and joyfully accept His promised forgiveness and clean slate (try using Ephesians 4:30-32 to guide your words).

You may need to run to Jesus because someone else was harsh towards you. If God is both just and merciful, how do you feel about Him showing gentleness towards those who hurt you?

How does Jesus confront and lift up Paul in Acts 9:3-6?

How does Paul later regard those who treated him poorly?

2 Timothy 4:16

Pray Matthew 6:9-13 and notice the only commentary Jesus gives on this prayer is in Matthew 6:14-15. Why do you think He emphasizes the importance of forgiveness?

Are you your own worst critic and let false accusations form your identity rather than relying on what God says about you? You may need to ask for God to forgive you for letting the enemy get a foothold in your life (Ephesians 4:27). Write a prayer and talk to God about it:

How do you feel after forgiving someone or yourself?

RISE

What are objects that you carry for long periods of time during the day? It might be a bag, a child, or a favorite cup of water. Next time you pick it up, think about how heavy the object feels. As you hold it for longer periods, does the perceived weight of the object change?

Compare this object to holding a grudge, and forgiveness to putting it down. Shame, guilt, and unforgiveness can be the source of our "heavy laden" sense of weariness. We may not even know how heavy it makes us feel until we let it go and rise up, feeling light as a feather.

Write a personal prayer for the day here, incorporating Proverbs 12:25: "Anxiety in a man's heart weighs it down, But a good word makes it glad."

Record anything else that comes to mind (a poem, a thought, a drawing):

What is one thing the Lord has taught you today that you will share with someone else? It can be wisdom in the form of words, compassion in the form of a hug, service in the form of meeting someone's need.

As you rise to your feet, invite the Spirit to rise within you.

DAY TWO

REST

Find a prayerful position, and fill in the prayer below:

Jesus,
Thank you for _____.

You are my _____ (i.e. Redeemer, Home, Hiding Place).

I give up my cares and plans to You today:

_____

_____

_____

Set a timer for eight minutes. Breathe deeply and release every muscle, starting from your toes and working up to your forehead. When your mind starts to wander like an ox for greener pastures, repeat Jesus's words, "for I am gentle and lowly in heart."

Let me rest my worth in your finished work. Let this offering of silence be pleasing to you, O Lord, my rock and my redeemer. Amen!

REFLECT

*"Come to me, all who labor and are heavy laden, and I will give you rest. Take my yoke upon you, and learn from me, **for I am gentle and lowly in heart**, and you will find rest for your souls."* Matthew 11:28-29

Write the verse below:

_____

_____

_____

_____

"...for I am gentle and lowly in heart..."

When I work for my own righteousness (being right in all things) or feel emotionally bruised, I need someone who is gentle and lowly. For me, the word "lowly" brings to mind a worm, the lowliest of creatures. Initially, I couldn't fathom any positive associations.

Worms are gross because they are slimy, squirmy, and almost shamefully naked. So, when David compares himself to a worm in Psalm 22:6, I take notice. David has been mocked, rejected, chased into caves, and feels like the lowest creature in the world. Worms are so low, they make their home in the dirt, the stuff we shake off shoes. But dirt is where the mustard seed grows.

Worms are crucial to plant growth. As they crawl in the deep, dark soil they create tunnels and aerate the ground, making space and allowing roots to find the nutrients they need. I tend to focus on how a plant looks above ground, but the important work is being done underground.

When you feel stuck or overwhelmed, it can be suffocating. How do you get a breath of fresh air and make space in your situation?

Our heart can often feel like an overbooked hotel: desires vying for a room by pushing, shoving, shouting, bribing, or cowering. Our heart is meant to be a home, a dwelling place for God, a space to sit at His feet.

"As the end approaches, there is no room for nature. The cities crowd it off the face of the earth. As the end approaches, there is no room for quiet. There is no room for solitude. There is no room for thought. There is no room for attention, for the awareness of our state. In the ultimate end, there is no room for man. Those that lament the fact that there is no room for God must also be called to account for this."
—Thomas Merton, The Time of No Room

When it came time for Jesus to be born into the world, there was no room in the inn. According to Isaiah 57:15, where does our High King live today?

What does He do there?

Can you name a time where you were in a low spot in life (financially, emotionally, relationally)? What or who brought you out?

Lysa Terkeurst explains the a difference between voluntarily humbling yourself and being humiliated: "one chose to bow low while the other fell there."[17]

Who is fully equipped to lift you up?

John 3:13

John 6:40

What must happen before we are raised?

---

[17] Lysa TerKeurst, *Uninvited: Living Loved When You Feel Less Than, Left Out, and Lonely* (Nashville: Harper Collins Publishing, 2016) 108.

John 12:24

1 Corinthians 15:42-43

What in your life do you need to let die?

What new life could Jesus bring out of it?

RISE

Jesus doesn't say, "Come to me, all who hustle and have great success!" He invites those who labor and are heavy laden, those who thirst for a cool drink of compassion from someone who cares. When you know you are in need, that is where Jesus is. It might be embarrassing to acknowledge weakness, but therein lies a space for God's strength, room to let Him grow us into our authentic self.

The Greek word for "lowly" is *tapeinós*, or God-reliant, which ironically means to exalt a person, or bring forth their true worth (1 Peter 5:6). What is one thing you have neglected that makes you feel completely you, fully alive, and overflowing with joy? Name one thing or person that makes you feel like you can rise above all the fears, doubts, and discouragement:

Write a prayer of supplication or praise incorporating Psalm 40:2. The prayer of supplication could be, "Jesus, please take me out of [insert low point] and let me praise you by [insert thing that gives you most joy]." The prayer of praise could be, "Jesus, thank you for reaching down and taking me out of _____; I am going to glorify you by [insert thing that gives you most joy]!"

Record anything else that comes to mind (a poem, a thought, a drawing):

"Kindness is a Christ-like attitude towards others, and humility is a Christ-like attitude towards oneself."—Trevor Joy[18]

What is one thing the Lord has taught you today that you will share with someone else? It can be wisdom in the form of words, compassion in the form of a hug, service in the form of meeting someone's need.

As you rise to your feet, invite the Spirit to rise within you.

---

[18] Trevor Joy, "Vivication," *The Village Church*, August 6, 2016, https://www.tvcresources.net/resource-library/sermons/vivification.

DAY THREE

REST

Find a prayerful position, and fill in the prayer below:

Jesus,

Thank you for _____.

You are my _____ (i.e. Way, Truth, Life).

I give up my cares and plans to You today:

_____

_____

_____

Set a timer for nine minutes. Breathe deeply and release every muscle, starting from your toes and working up to your forehead. When your mind starts to wander like an ox for greener pastures, repeat Jesus's words, "you will find rest for your souls."

Let me rest my worth in your finished work. Let this offering of silence be pleasing to you, O Lord, my rock and my redeemer. Amen!

REFLECT

*"Come to me, all who labor and are heavy laden, and I will give you rest. Take my yoke upon you, and learn from me, for I am gentle and lowly in heart, **and you will find rest for your souls.**"* Matthew 11:28-29

Write the verse below:

_____

_____

_____

_____

"...and you will find rest for your souls"

In this passage, Jesus is quoting from the Old Testament prophet Jeremiah: "Thus says the LORD: 'Stand by the roads, and look, and ask for the ancient paths, where the good way is; and walk in it, and find rest for your souls. But they said, 'We will not walk in it.'"[19]

This Scripture implies stopping and seeking out the best way to go. When our body detects a need like thirst, the brain will respond by identifying how to fulfill that need, mapping out the best way to get there, and assess any obstacles and risks along the way.[20] The reasonable choice would be to get a glass of water, but how many of us would choose coffee or sweet tea instead? Take a moment to assess your current physical and emotional needs: are you hungry or tired, jealous or

---

[19] Jeremiah 6:16
[20] Bessel van der Kolk, *The Body Keeps Score: Brain, Mind, and Body in Healing of Trauma* (New York: Penguin Books, 2015).

discouraged? How do you plan on fulfilling those needs?

Need   *Fulfillment*

_____   _____

_____   _____

_____   _____

The prophet Jeremiah acted as God's mouthpiece to entreat the people of Judah to put away their false idols to find rest in God's protection and avoid a Babylonian invasion. We may not be facing a Babylonian invasion, but we still face repercussions of disobeying God's Words of life.

Based on Judges 16, Biblical scholar Ravi Zacharias says this about separating from God's ways: "Sin will take you farther than you want to go, keep you longer than you want to stay, and cost you more than you want to pay." Describe how disobeying the Lord's commandments has affected the following in your life:

Taken you farther than you want to go:

Kept you longer than you want to stay:

Cost you more than you want to pay:

Even when we sin, God will restore everything the enemy has taken according to His merciful Name. Read Jeremiah 32:37-41 and write down what hits closest to home.

The "ancient paths" from Jeremiah 6:16 refers to the eternal ways—the shepherding by patriarchs, like Moses, of God's people into the promised land of rest and abundance. What does God say He will give the Israelites a few chapters later in Jeremiah 32:39?

How does God fulfill this promise in John 14:6?

Where does Matthew 11:29 above say we find rest?

John Koessler explains that the activity of rest doesn't always lead to the rest God intends for us: "Resting isn't rest any more than eating is food."[21] For example, we may eat, but junk food does not provide the best source of energy for our body. We may sleep, but it may not be the complete rest, the shalom, our soul needs. Only Jesus can provide the healthiest form of the rest we crave.

Sometimes when I'm feeling frustrated, I will open the pantry rather than pray to Jesus. But a full stomach does not calm a restless heart. By choosing food, I miss out on the bread of life. I know it's the wrong path, but it's the easy one. Jesus' way is a little harder—abstaining from the delights of the eyes is more difficult than walking by faith. But even so, He stands ready to for me to come back to Him.

How does your soul being at rest, being made right with God by Christ through faith, affect you? How does this compare with other options for earning rest?

How does the practice of seeking rest in Jesus affect your relationship with Him?

---

[21] John Koessler and Mark Galli in "The Radical Pursuit of Rest: Escaping the Productivity Trap" (Downers Grove: InterVarsity Press, 2016).

RISE

If you are able, go on a walk. When you go, consider your movement. To walk is to stick to it, to keep going, to put one foot in front of the other and let your body follow. When we come to a crossroads in decision making (whether that be on your actual walking path or in your day), let us thank Jesus for His cross, that He first chose us. Let us follow the gentle and humble voice that leads us on paths of righteousness.

Write out a prayer for the day here, incorporating Psalm 25:4-5.

Record anything else that comes to mind (a poem, a thought, a drawing):

What is one thing the Lord has taught you today that you will share with someone else? It can be wisdom in the form of words, compassion in the form of a hug, service in the form of meeting someone's need.

As you rise to your feet, invite the Spirit to rise within you.

RALLY

Recipe
Family Favorite Guacamole Recipe, makes 6 servings

I can't believe I'm divulging this family recipe with you. But since I have, I'll tell you the key to guacamole that stands apart from the rest: lime zest. You will need a microplane in your kitchen arsenal, my friends. The microplane is a tool that shreds the finest strands of the lime skin into the guacamole, giving it this citrusy punch that people will cock their heads and say, "What did you put in here?"

Ingredients:

- 4 avocados
- Zest and juice of one lime
- 2 tablespoons chopped cilantro
- 1 teaspoon sea salt
- 1 teaspoon onion powder

Directions:

Smash all ingredients together with a fork or potato masher, and serve with your choice of chips. You can use plantain chips to make this grain-free or go really wild and use crispy bacon strips to dip.

Prayer

Spend a moment in silence listening for the Lord to speak a different word to you, or say this prayer: *"Jesus, thank you for being gentle and humble enough to heed our prayers. Forgive us for the times we have hurt others and stubbornly refused to follow Your ways. By Your great mercy, lift us out of the quicksand of deception and set our feet upon the rock. We are tired of striving and yearn for higher ground. May we find rest in You alone."*

Icebreaker question: Would you rather ask someone for directions or say "I was wrong"?

Share your story: Do you struggle more with humility or gentleness? How has learning to be humble and gentle help you find inner rest?

What stuck out during this week's study? What does it say about you, God, and how can you apply it?

Let us be quick to confess and slow to anger. Use this time to humble yourself before the Lord and confess anything that has been weighing you down. Be lifted up by the collective words of the group: "He is faithful and just to forgive" (1 John 1:9).

Ending benediction. As you are able, get low (on your knees if you can), and say this prayer together:

"Jesus, may we find rest in You and rise with purpose. Amen!"

RECAP

Memory verse: "...for I am gentle and lowly in heart, and you will find rest for your souls." Matthew 11:29b

Message: Jesus bends low to gently give us the rest our soul craves.

Social Media Challenge: Find a plant that intrigues you and take a picture of it from an aerial view, fitting both the plant and the ground in the frame. You could say something like, "We often see the flower but dismiss the dirt. Today, I give thanks for humble beginnings. I may be [insert humble feature] but God has used it to [insert fruit of transformation]. Because out of the soil, out of a seed, God grew a miracle. We will rise from our roots!" #restandrisestudy

WEEK FOUR

Equipped for Encouragement

(Matthew 11:30)

DAY ONE

"He makes me lie down in green pastures..." I say, waiting for my three-year-old to repeat after me. She leaves me hanging, because she is hanging from her bunk bed ladder.

"Honey, please stop moving. Let's settle down. You need to sleep! We have a big day ahead of us."

You can lead a toddler to bed, but you can't make her nap. The fun-filled day is precisely why she doesn't want to lay down. She's too excited to try and learn how to say or practice Psalm 23, because she is looking forward to her first football game. A few hours later, my mother-in-law looks down and sees her snoring on her shoulder, right in the middle of the University of Georgia stadium. The next day, she develops a cough. The cough devolves into a fever, and the next thing you know, I'm stroking her hair as she sleeps in my lap.

Toddlers have just been introduced to this wonderful life and they don't want to miss a second. I occasionally catch the "fear of missing out" fever, but my reasons for staying up too long are not often for occasions like football games and Christmas Day, but racing the sun to get more work done before the day ends. I find myself seeking joy in accomplishments instead of Jesus, which never fulfills me like He can.

Thanks to electricity and email, we can work longer than the sun's rays. We can work on the bus, at a dance recital, in the middle of the night if we want to! But do we really get more done by working more? I believe this is a dangerous trend that will retroactively be viewed as outdated and unhealthy.

We know that taking time off is beneficial in more ways than one. In fact, "vacation improves health and well-being (82%), boosts morale (82%), and alleviates burnout (81%). Two-thirds of employees surveyed said their 'company culture is ambivalent, discouraging, or sends mixed messages about time off,' a share that's virtually unchanged since 2014."[22] According to this same article, 54% of Americans ended their year with vacation days. We may know that vacation and sleeping 7-9 hours is good for us, but mainstream American culture discourages breaks with incentivized workplaces, HR policies that police workday breaks, and some of the fewest vacation days of any developed nation.

When I make rest time a priority for my daughter I think, "I wish someone would tell me to rest in the middle of the day." Meanwhile, God's Word is standing there reminding me that He already does: "He makes me lie down" repeats Psalm 23.

Rest for the body is involuntary. Every human being on the face of the earth needs sleep. From Jeff Bezos to Jesus, every person requires daily physical rest. Death may be the great equalizer of man, but sleep is a daily external reminder of our internal need for rest.

Rest for the soul is voluntary. I can create a time of rest for my daughter, but I can't strong-arm her into sleeping. She is little and is still figuring out her body's signals for tiredness. However, even as adults we can miss our own body's signals if we are too busy: we can wake up with caffeine, easily cover up a sleep-deprived headache with Tylenol, and stay awake at

---

[22] Zillman, Claire. "Americans Are Still Terrible at Taking Vacations." Fortune. May 23, 2017. Accessed December 18, 2017. http://fortune.com/2017/05/23/vacation-time-americans-unused/.

night with artificial light. The same goes for our soul: we can alleviate stress with food, buy things to comfort us from burn-out, and stay busy to keep from collapsing.

God has built in plenty of physiological cues to alert us to weariness, but He doesn't force us to rest; He invites us to come to Him and allows us to learn from His gentle and humble ways. Whether we choose the hard way or Jesus' light and easy yoke is up to us.

REST

Find a prayerful position, settle in, and fill in the prayer below:

Jesus,
Thank you for _____.

You are my _____ (i.e. Shield, Lord of Hosts, Overcomer).

I give up my cares and plans to You today:

_____

_____

_____

Set a timer for ten minutes. Breathe deeply and release every muscle, starting from your toes and working up to your forehead. When your mind starts to wander like an ox for greener pastures, repeat Jesus's words, "For my yoke is easy, and my burden is light."

Let me rest my worth in your finished work. Let this offering of silence be pleasing to you, O Lord, my rock and my redeemer. Amen!

REFLECT

*"Come to me, all who labor and are heavy laden, and I will give you rest. Take my yoke upon you, and learn from me, for I am gentle and lowly in heart, and you will find rest for your souls. **For my yoke is easy, and my burden is light.**" Matthew 11:28-30*

Write the verse below:

_____

_____

_____

"For my yoke is easy, and my burden is light." Matthew 11:30

The word "easy" in Matthew 11:30 does not mean "without effort." The Greek has a wider range of meaning for the word—suitable, useful, properly productive, well-fitted, or beneficial. HELPS Word-Studies says this word "describes what God defines is kind – and therefore also eternally useful! We have no adjective in English that conveys this blend of being kind and good at the same time"[23]

I am slowly discovering what work is easy, or suitable, for who I am and what I have to offer. My top spiritual gift is teaching. My visual of a teacher is someone who stands on stage in front of thousands of people, spilling truth to the eager masses in a riveting voice that lifts the audience to their feet shouting "Preach it, sister!"

---

[23] HELPS Word-studies copyright 1987, 2011 by Helps Ministries, Inc. For complete text and additional resources visit: TheDiscoveryBible.com.

The notoriety and influence of a stage is attractive, but it is not my natural bent. Instead of being a "captivating celebrity," my personality test revealed behind-the-scenes words like "low dominance," "observer," and "listener." Knowing how God made me gave me permission to stop pursuing stardom and start doing what came easy—writing Bible studies and facilitating groups. These are not easy because the work is easy (I typically use every brain cell to write and all of my attentive energy to listen), but because these assignments fit with my passion and personality.

Read 1 Samuel 17:38-39. What happened when David wore the King's armor?

What does he put on instead? See 1 Samuel 17:40.

Describe a time when you felt you needed to live up to an expectation that did not feel right for you. As David chose what fit him best, did you switch out the cumbersome suit of armor for something more suitable?

What did you exchange?

Goliath charges into battle with a giant sword, spear, and javelin. What is David armed with (see 1 Samuel 17:45)?

Is this enough for you?

The Israelites and the Philistines had been in a stalemate for months, but David secured a swift victory. Talk about a memory of work that seemed to fly by:

Now, write down an experience that seemed to drag its feet:

What is the difference between the two?

There are two Greek words for time: chronos and kairos. To put it succinctly, chronos measures minutes and kairos observes moments. There is chronological time, and there is the way we experience time. In the Old Testament days, Jacob served his father-in-law for seven years to win Rachel's hand in marriage. What does Genesis 29:20 say is the reason it only felt like a few days?

When work is hard, our eyes are on the clock, counting down until quitting time. When work is easy, our eyes are on the reward. Our work can be as daunting as facing a giant or as long as spending 14 years in an unpaid job (shoutout to all the parents). Jesus' heavy work was to take on all the sins of the world. What motivated Him to keep moving towards Jerusalem? See Hebrews 12:2.

This easy yoke of Christ, also spoken about as the cross, refers to John 13:34: "A new commandment I give to you, that you love one another: just as I have loved you, you also are to love one another." Read Leviticus 19:18. How is John 13:34 a new commandment? Think about who is speaking in each Scripture.

Jesus' burden is easy because He is the one who fulfills it. He gives us rules not as a restriction but as a fitting frame for our finite selves. Paul Brand, in his book *Fearfully and Wonderfully Made*, compares our bones to the law: they allow the body freedom to move—until one is broken. Write down how the writers of this Bible viewed the law:

Psalm 119:174

1 John 5:3

"Christ's yoke is like feathers to a bird; not loads, but helps tomotion."—Jeremy Taylor [24]

In John 16:33 Jesus says, "I have said these things to you, that in me you may have peace. In the world you will have tribulation. But take heart; I have overcome the world." The world may not get easier, but in Christ, our hearts become lighter. Circle or highlight the verse below that speaks most to you:

> but they who wait for the LORD shall renew their strength;
> they shall mount up with wings like eagles;
> they shall run and not be weary;
> they shall walk and not faint.
> —Isaiah 40:31

---

[24] Taylor, Meremy and Thomas Smart Hughes in *The Works of Jeremy Taylor*, Volume 2 (A.J. Valpy, 1832) 154.

Let me dwell in your tent forever! Let me take refuge under the shelter of your wings! Selah —Psalm 61:4

And let us not grow weary of doing good, for in due season we will reap, if we do not give up. —Galatians 6:9

The light shines in the darkness, and the darkness has not overcome it. —John 1:5

RISE

Let's try something together. Turn up the corners of your mouth into a smile. Did anything around you change? Did the trash take itself out, or the paper write itself? More importantly, did anything inside of you change?

As the muscles of our mouth lift into a smile, may the Lord be the lifter of our heart. Let us count all our trials and toiling as joy, for joy is not a byproduct of success—it is a pure and holy gift from God through Christ. No matter what our job title is, let us be occupied with joy[25].

Write out a prayer for the day here. Ask the Lord for the faith and strength to live out 2 Peter 1:5-8 to keep you from being ineffective or unfruitful in the knowledge of Christ.

---

[25] Ecclesiastes 5:20

Record anything else that comes to mind (a poem, a thought, a drawing):

What is one thing the Lord has taught you today that you will share with someone else? It can be wisdom in the form of words, compassion in the form of a hug, or service in the form of meeting someone's need.

As you rise to your feet, invite the Spirit to rise within you.

DAY TWO

REST

Find a prayerful position, settle in, and fill in the prayer below:

Jesus,
Thank you for _____.

You are my _____ (i.e. Strength, Encourager, Giver of Grace).

I give up my cares and plans to You today:

_____

_____

_____

Set a timer for eleven minutes. Breathe deeply and release every muscle, starting from your toes and working up to your forehead. When your mind starts to wander like an ox for greener pastures, repeat Jesus's words, "For my yoke is easy, and my burden is light."

Let me rest my worth in your finished work. Let this offering of silence be pleasing to you, O Lord, my rock and my redeemer. Amen!

REFLECT

"Come to me, all who labor and are heavy laden, and I will give you rest. Take my yoke upon you, and learn from me, for I am gentle and lowly in heart, and you will find rest for your souls. **For my yoke is easy, and my burden is light***."* Matthew 11:28-30

Write the verse below:

_____

_____

_____

_____

"For my yoke is easy, and my burden is light." Matthew 11:30

I recall watching a television character struggle over a moral dilemma. On each shoulder stood a representation for good or evil. A man robed in white recited the right thing to do, while the opposite dressed in black leather played the devil's advocate. Meanwhile, the character listened to the back and forth crossfire, distraught over the tough decision. I haven't seen this visual depicted in any popular media recently, and I wonder if it is because our culture fiercely protects the right to be right in our own eyes.

Nonetheless, we each have a highly unique set of burdens that live in our conscience—but instead of an angel on one shoulder and the devil on the other, it's our faith in one hand and our flesh in the other. Choosing between the two can wear us out, especially when we want to do what's right.

Romans 14:23b says, "whatever does not proceed from faith is sin." Our burden of conscience proceeds from our level of faith. The Romans 14 passage speaks to the age-old conviction of vegetarians versus meat eaters, but we could also turn to other provocative issues such as the mode of baptism, the presence of God in communion, or controversial methods of loading the dishwasher.

The Greek word Jesus uses for burden is *phortion* – a burden or freight of a ship which is deeply personal and non-transferable. It must be carried by the individual and cannot be given to another. This is the same word used in Galatians 6:5: "For each will have to bear his own load." Each person is responsible for his or her own sins, conscious and hidden.

In John 8:1-11, the scribes and Pharisees carried a heavy load of rocks to bury the woman already heavy with shame. How does Jesus redirect their ammunition?

How does Jesus empower the woman to go forth in honor of his pardon?

Who does Romans 14:4 say can make us stand on judgement day?

We are each individual servants of the same Lord. We each have our own load to carry and responsibility to act on our faith. In 1 Corinthians 15:9, at the beginning of his ministry, Paul compares his heavy load to those around him and calls himself the "least of the apostles." By the end of his ministry, he claims to be the "chief of sinners" (1 Timothy 1:15). How does walking with Jesus by faith change Paul's view of his own sin?

How does it change his view of Jesus?

The longer we walk with Jesus, the more apparent our sin becomes. But where sin abounds, grace abounds even more.

There are the burdens of sins of commission and the burdens of sins of omission. James 4:17 says, "So whoever knows the right thing to do and fails to do it, for him it is sin."

Imagine this day with me. You open your phone in the morning to breaking news headlines that break your heart: "300 Gunned Down in Egypt," "Human Trafficking on the Rise," and "Tsunami Wipes Out 3,000 Homes." You go into work and get the news that your boss is out because he has cancer. You head to the grocery store and the cashier informs you of the food bank shortage and asks you to donate. Later, at your church small group you listen to twenty minutes of prayer requests, but the time ends and you forget to actually pray for them. You collapse into bed, feeling the weight of the world and the heaviness of your eyelids. They close, and you wake up again, feeling gravity grow stronger overnight.

You want to help, but the broken weariness of the world is overwhelming.

1 Peter 5:7 encourages us to cast all our anxieties on the Lord, because He cares for us. Instead of receiving a burden of compassion and carrying it around all day, how can you fulfill this verse in the moment you receive some difficult news? See 1 Thessalonians 5:17.

Galatians 6:5 says we must carry our own load, but what is the law of Christ according to Galatians 6:2? Listen to the song *When the Saints* by Sara Groves for theme music.

We don't have to be God to change the whole world—but we can let God change our world. Let's give what we have been given. Write down how you have been loved, and how you can lift up another's burden in the same way:

How you have been loved   *How you can love another*

_____   _____

_____   _____

_____   _____

Jesus says His burden is light, and His command to love others as we have been loved is easy work. The word "light" Jesus used in Matthew 11:30 also occurs in 2 Corinthians 4:17. Write this verse:

How does this verse change your perspective on today's burdens?

RISE

If you are in a position to stand, go ahead and do so. Now, bend your knees and slowly send your hips back like you are going to sit in a chair, but hover about two inches from the chair.

After ten seconds, take a seat.

Which felt harder—using your own body to support yourself, or sitting down in faith that the chair would hold you?

Jesus is like the chair. When we bring our whole self to Him, he will support us. We still need to activate the muscles of our core to keep us upright, but in comparison to resting in our own strength, it is a light burden. Jesus is our place of rest.

Write out a prayer for the day, incorporating Deuteronomy 32:11, thanking the Lord for bearing you up.

Record anything else that comes to mind (a poem, a thought, a drawing):

What is one thing the Lord has taught you today that you will share with someone else? It can be wisdom in the form of words, compassion in the form of a hug, service in the form of meeting someone's need.

As you rise to your feet, invite the Spirit to rise within you.

DAY THREE

REST

Assume a posture of surrender, and fill in the prayer below:

Jesus,
Thank you for _____.

You are my _____ (i.e. Freedom, Strength, Sword).

I give up my cares and plans to You today:

_____

_____

_____

Set a timer for twelve minutes. Breathe deeply and release every muscle, starting from your toes and working up to your forehead. When your mind starts to wander like an ox for greener pastures, repeat Jesus's words, "For my yoke is easy, and my burden is light."

Let me rest my worth in your finished work. Let this offering of silence be pleasing to you, O Lord, my rock and my redeemer. Amen!

REFLECT

"Come to me, all who labor and are heavy laden, and I will give you rest. Take my yoke upon you, and learn from me, for I am gentle and lowly in heart, and you will find rest for your souls. For my yoke is easy, and my burden is light." Matthew 11:28-30

Write the verse below:

_____

_____

_____

_____

"For my yoke is easy, and my burden is light." Matthew 11:30

In Luke 13, Jesus heals a woman in the synagogue on the Sabbath and sends the Pharisees into a frenzy. They firmly remind him that no work is allowed on the Sabbath. Jesus responds, "'You hypocrites! Does not each of you on the Sabbath untie his ox or his donkey from the manger and lead it away to water it? And ought not this woman, a daughter of Abraham whom Satan bound for eighteen years, be loosed from this bond on the Sabbath day?'" (Luke 13:15-16) This woman has a chance to be healed, and the Pharisees tell her to come back another day—apparently to them, the Lord's day is not for freedom.

This woman was crooked in stature, her back so bent it could not be straightened, as if she was bending under an invisible load. She didn't let her handicap stop her. She found a way to get to the temple and seek solace in her God. Jesus saw her infirmity, broke the yoke of Satan so she could stand upright for the first time in eighteen years, and all the Pharisees can say is, "You can't do that." Way to rain on this miracle parade, Pharisees.

Jesus takes the stones out of their hypocritical satchels by pointing out how the Pharisees lead their ox or donkey out for water on the Sabbath, the same animals they use for work. If God created the Sabbath, and only God has the power to recreate, or make new what has been broken, then Jesus must be God. But this Pharisee who spoke against Jesus did not repent. He refused to admit he was wrong. One might say he was as stubborn as a mule.

Jesus is in the business of loving people, even if that means doing business on the day of rest. He is Lord of the Sabbath, and defines it as a day to lift burdens. In doing so, we might find that another type of burden has been lifted from us. He teaches us how to rest God's way.

What does Ezekiel 20:12 say is God's purpose for the Sabbath?

How do you practice Sabbath?

Shelly Miller, author of the book *Rhythms of Rest*, explains observing the Sabbath is doing anything that is "easy and light."[26] What is easy and light for you?

I started observing a whole Sabbath day in college when I felt constant pressure to spend any free time studying. I reserved Saturdays for doing anything "easy and light," with no obligations outside my ordinary responsibilities. I needed one day to simply enjoy, and not strive over, God's creation. I cooked, read fiction, took long walks—all things I enjoyed but did not have time for during the week. At first, it was hard to refrain from doing what I "should" do. What does Leviticus 23:32 say to do during this period of solemn rest?

How does Jesus describe walking on the path to life in Matthew 7:14?

---

[26] Heather MacFayden, "Thinking Differently About Sabbath :: Shelly Miller [EP 101}," *God Centered Mom Blog*, October 16, 2017, http://godcenteredmom.com/2017/10/16/thinking-differently-about-sabbath-shelly-miller-ep-181.

The way is hard—pulling away from the tension to complete and compete in an internet-based society is difficult. How does Nehemiah protect the Sabbath in Nehemiah 13:19?

Observing and guarding a period of time to practice putting on Jesus' easy yoke and light burden primes us for a Sabbath heart. A Sabbath heart is one that finds rest even in work.

Hebrews 4:10-11 says this, "for whoever has entered God's rest has also rested from his works as God did from his. Let us therefore strive to enter that rest, so that no one may fall by the same sort of disobedience."

McLaren explains in his commentary:

"The 'rest' which Genesis speaks about was, of course, not repose that recruited exhausted strength, but the cessation of work because the work was complete, the repose of satisfaction in what we should call an accomplished ideal...And, further, the rest of God is compatible with, and, indeed, but another form of, unceasing activity. 'My Father worketh hitherto, and I work,' said the Master; though the works were, in one sense, finished from the foundation of the world."[27]

---

[27] "Hebrews 4:11," *Bible Hub*, accessed November 15th, 2017, http://biblehub.com/commentaries/hebrews/4-11.htm.

The way is hard, but the work is easy. Our traditional view of work is to labor *for* victory—but Jesus works *from* victory. The reward has been won! All there is left to do is walk on the winning side of eternity. The end is determined and the unstoppable plan of salvation has been set in motion and accomplished on the cross. Denying our own passions and pleasures is difficult, but Jesus promises that when we pick up His yoke, the work will be easy.

There will be no sense of striving to make ends meet because Jesus is the provider.

There will be no sense of striving in our work to complete a task because Jesus will finish the work He started in us.

There will be no sense of striving in our work to gain recognition because Jesus sees our hidden parts and loves us fully.

Are you working for rest or from rest?

Aside from life-and-death work, do you feel like you're unable to take a break from any area of work in your life?

What would happen if you did stop that work for a period?

How do you think God could meet your needs during that time?

How would this build up your faith in Him?

Take this answer and apply it to everything you do. When you are lacking confidence, time, energy, or skill, rest and let God arise from the void and do the impossible. After all, He did create the heavens and the earth out of nothing. Think of what He could do with your empty hands! When we give up our lifeand can truly say, "all I have is Christ," *then* we have everything we need, plus more to give away.

RISE

Try holding your breath for 10 seconds. What feelings rise up in you? What are you desperate for?

Let us be as desperate for Jesus as for the air in our lungs. When our vital functions cease even for a second, we wake up to our intense need for oxygen. We remember how little attention we pay to all the things that go right until something goes wrong. We notice that God is in control of more than we thought, we are more indebted to His love than we knew, and it's okay to take a break because He has everything under control. And when we do rest from our work, may it grow a craving for His life-giving presence.

Read Psalm 121 and replace the "you" with "me," making it a personal conversation between you and the Lord. Write out this prayer of trust in God for the day:

Record anything else that comes to mind (a poem, a thought, a drawing):

What is one thing the Lord has taught you today that you could share with someone else? It can be wisdom in the form of words, compassion in the form of a hug, service in the form of meeting someone's need.

As you rise to your feet, invite the Spirit to rise within you.

RALLY

Recipe
Gluten-Free Cinnamon Bun Bread

Let's go big for this last recipe and incorporate the process of resting and rising with delicious cinnamon swirl bread! You will need to give yourself about three hours for the finished product, but you will only spend about 20 active minutes in the kitchen.

Ingredients:
- 3 cups all purpose gluten-free flour
- 3 tablespoons sugar
- 2 teaspoons instant yeast
- 1 1/4 teaspoons salt
- 1 1/4 teaspoons xantham gum
- 1 cup warm milk of choice
- 4 tablespoons melted coconut oil
- 3 large eggs

Cinnamon filling
- 3 tablespoons melted coconut oil
- 1/3 cup brown sugar
- 1 1/2 tablespoons ground cinnamon

Directions:
Using an electric mixer, combine first five ingredients. Then with mixer running on low, slowly pour in warm milk until combined. Add coconut oil until combined, then mix in eggs. Beat on high speed for three minutes until smooth. Cover the bowl and let the batter rise for one hour.

Mix cinnamon filling ingredients.

Once the dough has risen, grease a 9" x 5" bread pan. Scoop half the dough into the pan, then layer with cinnamon filling. Top with the other half of the dough. If desired, sprinkle the top of the bread with cinnamon sugar for an extra crunch.

Cover the pan with plastic wrap and let the dough rise until it is within 1" from the top of the wrap, about 45 to 60 minutes. Preheat the oven to 350 °F during the last 15-20 minutes of the rise.

Bake at 350 °F for 38 to 42 minutes until a beautiful golden brown.

When you get together, make a big ceremony of it by blessing the food, holding the loaf above your head and breaking it in half to shouts of "hooray!"

PRAYER

Spend a moment in silence listening for the Lord to speak a different word to you, or say this prayer:

"Lord, we don't deserve You. You took our burdens on the cross so we would never have to carry them again. How sweet is your grace! Let us receive it with open hands. Let us drop our own burdens of sin and expectations in exchange for faith that You carry us on wings like eagles. Let us take comfort in the shelter of Your wings. Send us out with well-fitted armor of God as we carry a torch of light in a dark world. In Jesus' name, amen."

Icebreaker question: Would you rather wear shoes two sizes too big for a day or carry a 40-pound pack for three hours?

Share your story: What is your understanding of the Sabbath? Do you practice it now? If so, what does it look like? How do you hope Sabbath will look in your life?

What stuck out during this week's study? What does it say about you, God, and how can you apply it?

Spend a minute going around the circle, confirming each person's innate and individual strength for serving others. Instruct each person to answer with, "I receive it." Then, give them time to answer how they can use that gift to bear up someone else's burden.

For example:

"Suzie, you are good at listening," says one person in the group.

Suzie responds, "Thank you; I receive it! I could ask my employees for feedback and really take time to listen."

Ending benediction. Gently lift up your neighbor's right wrist and say this prayer together, "Jesus, may we find rest in You and rise with purpose. Amen!"

RECAP

Memory verse: "For my yoke is easy, and my burden is light." — Matthew 11:30

Message: Jesus equips to encourage others.

Social Media Challenge: Take a picture of you in your element, doing what comes easy and joyful, with this quote attached: "The place God calls you to is the place where your deep gladness and the world's deep hunger meet."—Frederick Buechner #restandrisestudy

EPILOGUE

Wow, thank you for sojourning with me! May this leg of your journey be one to refresh you on your way to our heavenly country.

My prayer is that you would find real rest in Jesus, and that He would give you eyes to see the harvest. A clear vision makes for an unstoppable drive to the finish.

As we rest, rise, and repeat, we will see the path unroll before us:

A man buys a field and appoints servants to work in it. The man gives instructions to let the ground lay fallow after six years. He promises to provide everything the servants need during the seventh year there is no food from the ground. The servants abuse the field by not letting it rest, so the soil is depleted of nutrients. Henceforth, everything the ground grows tastes more bland and gives less nourishment. The servants turn to other synthetic vitamins for their strength and keep working, producing less and feeling more tired and frustrated.

The owner of the field sends his own son to show them how he wants the work to be done. Instead of striving in the soil like the servants expect, he takes time to heal the servants who have been wounded by the heavy labor and discouragement. The servants are angry. They take the son and kill him, hoping to get rid of this new nuisance and take his inheritance.

The son does not stay in the ground. The soil, as if in an act of worship and obedience to its Maker, lifts him up and restores him to the father. Only those recognize they labor and are heavy laden see, and the rest of the workers disbelieve. The believers walk in the ways of the Son, helping those who have fallen behind, instead of trying to get ahead, spreading this new way of life through every act of love.

In the end, the believers follow the son back to the owner of the field, who makes all things new. The owner of the field reveals the harvest that he has been storing in heaven, the harvest the believers reaped by sowing their efforts in the way of the son. The fruit is unity out of discord, laughter out of tears, transformation out of trauma, peace out of pain, running out of crawling. The fruit is a forever feast with multitudes of the faithful. They no longer need to work for their survival, for the son is their forever sustenance.

APPENDIX A: CELEBRATE

L et's celebrate what you have gained over the past four weeks with the following questions (answers are located on the bottom):

1. How do we get rest for our soul?
A.) Sit back and wait
B.) Go to Jesus
C.) Sleep until we feel better

2. Who did Jesus invite to come to Him?
A.) People who have it all together
B.) People who are weary of the world and work
C.) Those who don't need help
D.) The rich and famous

3. What is a yoke?
A.) The yellow part of an egg
B.) A furry animal with horns
C.) A wooden crossbar connecting two animals, attached to a plow or cart

4. What's the next step after taking Jesus' yoke?
A.) Put your head down and work hard
B.) Quit your job and become a pastor
C.) Learn from Jesus

5. How does Jesus describe Himself?

_____ and _____ in heart

6. What kind of rest does Jesus offer?

_____

7. True or false: when I start walking with Jesus, He will carry everything and I can enjoy the ride.

8. Write Matthew 11:28-30:

At the beginning of the study, you wrote down what you hoped to gain from this study. Refer back to your answer and record it here.

What are three things you learned or benefited from in this study?

1.

2.

3.

What is one takeaway point you can put into action today?

I will _____

ANSWER KEY

1. B
2. B
3. C
4. C
5. Gentle and humble
6. Soul rest, or rest for the whole being (body, spirit, soul)
7. False
8. "Come to me, all who labor and are heavy laden, and I will give your rest. Take my yoke upon you and learn from me, for I am gentle and humble and heart, and you will find rest for your souls. For my yoke is easy, and my burden is light." Matthew 11:28-30

How will you continue meeting together as Hebrew 10:24 encourages us to do? It could be another Bible study or just a regular time to get together with like-minded brothers and sisters. Write it out here:

I highly encourage you to dig into your local church community. Jesus made the effort to visit us in person, so we need to value face-to-face relationships and reserve the digital world as a highway to foster fellowship around the world.

If you would like to continue this journey online, join the *Rest and Rise Collective* by subscribing with your email address in the link below. I will send you resources and tips to encourage rest in Jesus and equip you to rise in purpose with the people around you. I don't want this email to add to your to-do list stress. Please, only open an email from me if it gives you rest and helps you rise!

Subscribe: kaseybshuler.com/join

Tag #restandrise on social media

Will You Help Me Choose?

Thank you so much for going through this study. I fully appreciate you taking the time to read these words, and honor your feedback.

I need your input to make the next version better.

Please head on over to Amazon and leave a helpful review. Help me choose what stays in, and what needs to go. Let's write the next one together!

With gratitude,

Kasey Shuler

APPENDIX B:
LEADER GUIDE

The best leader is a follower of Jesus.

To lead a group through this book you don't need to be a deacon or have a degree in seminary, but good leaders are under leadership to Jesus and a local church.

Leading a group is less about having the answers and more about pointing to the One who does have the answers.

Leading a group is less about talking and more about listening.

Leading a group is less about finishing the questions and more about facilitating a safe community where people feel loved.

The best way to be this leader is to rest and rise:

If you feel anxious about people coming over your house, stop and rest. It's not the house that makes a safe space. Jesus dwells within you! Be at peace with Him in the space of your body, so you can be welcoming arms to others.

If someone shares something deep and beyond the scope of your care, take a moment and rest by praying as a group for that person, then follow-up with them afterwards. Have local counseling resources on hand in case you need extra help.

If one person dominates the time and others don't get to share, consider suggesting a ten-second silence after each question. You could emphasize that resting in silence is necessary for growth—both for the one who feels like he needs to fill the space and for the one who needs that space to formulate his thoughts.

ORGANIZING A GROUP STUDY

Reach out to your church leadership and share your desire to lead a group through this study, asking for prayers and support.

You can direct them to
kaseybshuler.com/shop/restandrisestudy to learn more.

1. Pray about who you would like to invite. List their names here:

   _____   _____   _____

   _____   _____   _____

   _____   _____   _____

   _____   _____   _____

2. Ask them if they would be interested in going through the study. You may use the any promotional materials on kaseybshuler.com/shop/restandrisestudy.

3. Determine a time that works best for everyone for five weeks (the last week is the Celebration week). You'll need about an hour and a half to *Rally*.

4. Secure a place to meet where you will be able to pray and discuss personal details safely. Think through the following: Will you need childcare? Do you have sufficient seating or are you doing a walking study group? Is there a plan B if

your location falls through?

5. Provide resources: Order enough books for the group. You might need a few extra in case anyone joins in late.

6. Think about your Celebration Week. This is a time to celebrate the past month together and discuss next steps of how to continue meeting in community, whether that's with the same group or another. You could celebrate by hosting a potluck, having a dance party, or go out for a treat. You could celebrate by serving the community and volunteer at a local nursing home or food bank (plan this ahead of time). You could combine the two and have people bring canned goods or new/gently used clothes as an "entry fee" and donate them after the get together. Get creative!

SUGGESTIONS FOR THE GATHERING

- If there are more than two people in a group, assign prayer partners. The role of the prayer partner is to follow-up and pray with or for the other person at least once a week. Prayer partners provide support and accountability throughout the study.

- Meet once before the study begins over coffee, tea, a hike outside, or whatever the group prefers so everyone will feel more comfortable sharing during the first week of the study. Go over the expectations and read them out loud together:

  1. The group is a place to feel safe and loved.

  2. We don't need to fix each other. We get to listen and let the Lord do His work.

  3. Everything shared stays within the group.

4. God is after our hearts. He waits on us. We get to reciprocate by showing up, doing the work, and being honest.

- Be willing to go first. Whatever you share first will set the bar for how vulnerable others will be.

- Assign the first week's study and then plan a time to gather together and share what each person has learned from that week using the Rally section at the end of each week.

- Follow-up with the group. You may use the *Recap* at the end of each week or just send them a message to say you're thinking about them and looking forward to seeing them again!

ACKNOWLEDGEMENTS

"**I**n all your ways acknowledge him, and he will make straight your paths." Proverbs 3:6

To acknowledge is to make what is hidden known, to recognize someone's contributions and take notice of the impact. You may be reading these words, but what you do not know is how many people have influenced, supported, and made this study better than I ever could have. All good things take a village!

First and foremost to Jesus, who has been teaching me to rest my whole life without one word of acknowledgement from me. Thank you for persevering and pursuing me. I'm finally starting to see the light...even with my eyes closed.

To my mom, without whom this book's idea would not have existed, and without whom I would not have existed. Thank you for spurring me on towards love and good deeds and supporting me in every single thing I do, no matter how many times I change my mind.

To my husband, who sees me better than I see myself. You not only challenge me to follow my dreams, but make a way for me to pursue them. Thank you for sacrificing sleep and taking care of our little girl to allow me time write, and for postponing *Brooklyn 99* until I meet my deadlines.

To Teresa, my women's health physical therapist. You set me on the path to healing.

To my editor and friend, Danielle. Thank you for challenging me to write this study, and for making room in your life to see it through and make it better than I ever could. You were with me at the start of my writing journey, and I look forward to more!

To Julie, Danielle, Lydia, Ashton, Heather, and Katie. Thank you for your feedback and being my testers, or bfs (Beta Friends).

To Lindsey, my friend and writing accountability colleague. Your uplifting and generous spirit is more valuable than you know.

To Allison, my friend and skilled wordsmith. Thank you for editing a book that I never published. Your editing advice still rings in my ears as I write.

OTHER RESOURCES FROM KASEY

Move for Joy

If you've ever felt bad about not exercising or haven't found the right workout for you, Move for Joy will help you stop starting over. By connecting your fitness journey with the joy of Jesus, this book will help you put together a sustainable workout guide that supports your life, how you were made to move, and what you truly enjoy.

The Lord's Prayer: A 12-Week Journal

Not sure how to pray? This journal breaks down the Lord's prayer into morning and evening templates for a week, starting with the a Sabbath day and ending with free-writing pages. Including prompts to pray for each group of people in your life, this journal will help give you focus in the way Jesus taught us to pray.

Love Beyond Looks

Your body changes, but God's love for you will not! In this 5-week study, you'll discover how God sees you and loves you as you are through the mirror of His Word.

Learn more at kaseybshuler.com/shop

Made in the USA
Las Vegas, NV
28 February 2023

68290413R00089